DISCARD

S0-BDL-550

HOW TO TEACH
ENGLISH TO FOREIGNERS

BY

HENRY H. GOLDBERGER

Principal Public School 18, Manhattan, New York City
Instructor Methods of Teaching English to Foreigners, Teachers College, Columbia
Director Americanization Institute New York City

NOV 1 2 2008

Lucius E. and
Elsie C. Burch, Jr. Library
501 Poplar View Pkwy
Collierville, TN 38017

Copyright 1918
BY HENRY H. GOLDBERGER
All rights reserved.

In the interest of creating a more extensive selection of rare historical book reprints, we have chosen to reproduce this title even though it may possibly have occasional imperfections such as missing and blurred pages, missing text, poor pictures, markings, dark backgrounds and other reproduction issues beyond our control. Because this work is culturally important, we have made it available as a part of our commitment to protecting, preserving and promoting the world's literature. Thank you for your understanding.

THE AIMS IN TEACHING ENGLISH TO FOREIGNERS

The absence of pedagogic theory and of a medium for discussing the teaching of English to foreigners have helped to retain and to recapitulate practices after they had outlived their usefulness. Particularly is this true where guidance in the selection of content and method is lacking because of an uncertain aim. Teachers of children, unless otherwise directed, tend to carry over their pedagogic theory to the teaching of adults; lay teachers tend to reproduce vaguely remembered snatches of their own school days; rarely is the psychology of the adult foreigner taken into account in planning instruction for him. Teachers of English to foreign adults have not been conscious of a definite aim or goal in terms both of English and the special needs of the pupils. Such general aims as:

to Americanize the foreigner
to teach him to read the newspaper
to read English literature
to become an American citizen
to understand America
to train him in civics
to teach him correct pronunciation

do not serve as a guide in the selection of content and of method.

For social, economic and psychological reasons non-English speaking peoples tend to settle near each other and to occupy distinct sections of cities and towns and to perpetuate their old world customs and language. English speaking Americans accent this isolation by moving out when foreigners come in. Thus there have been created The Little Italys, the Little Hungarys the Little Bohemias in our American cities. Within these foreign sections the foreign resident finds no need for acquiring a knowledge of English. He buys and sells by using his native tongue. He reads his newspapers printed in his native language. Frequently moving pictures and the drama are presented in his language and a generous America through the public library furnishes books in the language which he reads. At work, the American employers in their eagerness to secure labor provide foremen and superintendents who can communicate their wishes in the foreign language of the laborer. The latter becomes a member of a Union, of a club or of a fraternal organization composed of his fellow countrymen, and again no compelling reason exists for the arduous labor required in learning English. He worships the God of freedom and is exhorted to walk in the ways of his fathers in the language which he first learned at the feet of his mother. In brief, all his needs, material, cultural and spiritual are satisfied with-

1

out a knowledge of the language of America and rarely does he consciously set out to acquire it. In their infrequent contact with English speaking people at work or in their occasional transgressions beyond the confines of the section in which they live, the man and the working woman pick up a number of English words or sentences, which by frequent use they come to regard as part of their native equipment and to pronounce on the basis of a phonetic system totally foreign. But the woman, weighed down by household cares, has even this limited opportunity for coming in contact with English speaking people denied her and realizes her need only when an impassable gulf has opened between her and her children who have learned to speak English in the public schools and then she is ashamed or too old to go to school.

The unusually energetic, those filled with ambition, with a thirst for knowledge or with a direct need for English in self advancement, in business, in acquiring citizenship, enter classes to overcome their deficiency. They learn under great hardships, after a day of toil, frequently insufficiently nourished, robbing themselves of leisure hours. Each remains under instruction only so long as he considers the instruction worth while—only so long as the return is commensurate with his sacrifice.

The usual aims and values ascribed to content and procedure in teaching children, lack validity for the immigrant whose Americanization is to begin by learning English. He does not desire a knowledge of English to acquire a culture of the ornamental kind, to be disciplined in thinking or to have his memory trained; he is skeptical of future returns to be acquired by present hardships. His needs are present and urgent; he is impatient to use what he learns today and to meet future needs as they arise. Needless to say his psychology is sound. Not only is the satisfaction of present needs the surest means toward holding the interest of the pupil in the present but it is the only guarantee that subsequent needs will be met as effectively in the future. The foreigner who finds the instruction in English worth while today because he can apply it at once outside of the class room will tomorrow return because a new problem has presented itself. In brief, the point of departure in teaching English to foreigners cannot be certain conventional aims and values found in the subject matter called "English" or in processes of teaching, but must be found in the pupils themselves. Since they are free agents to come if they like or to go if they choose—per diem pupils—the question "what is worth while," is of even greater importance in such instruction than it is with children who are compelled to attend for fixed periods or with High School or College students who voluntarily enter upon instruction to continue for fixed periods. The latter students might be compared to guests at a banquet—expected to remain from hors d'oeuvre to demi-tasse, to taste a little of each dish presented and to rise when the hostess rises. Foreigners who seek

2

English instruction, however, are rather like the patrons of buffet lunches—they have time and money for only a few solid dishes but they may be tempted to try a dessert by the quality and the price of the food.

In considering the question "What is worth while" for foreigners learning English, it is well to bear in mind the two-fold purpose in teaching English; 1st, to communicate thoughts; 2nd, to acquire the thoughts of others. The first is a problem largely of teaching conversation, the second a problem in teaching a pupil to read. An insight into the psychology of the foreign pupil may be obtained by imagining an American in Russia or in Greece laboring under the same difficulties as those under which foreigners labor in America and handicapped by a similar lack of knowledge of the language of the country. Such an American would primarily want to learn as much of the langauge of the country as will enable him to make his way, to understand the natives, to be understood by them, and only secondarily, to read their literature, their constitutions and declarations of independence. In other words, he would desire a knowledge of the language to communicate his thoughts rather than to read the thoughts of others, and if he analyzed his own state of mind and were not numbed into acquiescence by the authority of the teacher, he would realize that he required to talk in Russian not in such terms as he would use in speaking to his English speaking friends in Russia, but such Russian sentences and on such topics as would enable him to get along with Russians who spoke no English; any old Russian words would not do, least of all archaic, pedantic or technically political locutions. Moreover, language teachers know that speaking precedes reading and writing and is besides the psychological basis for the teaching of visual symbols in association with auditory symbols acquired in oral language. On pain of refusing to remain a pupil but of course without giving utterance to the unconscious thought, the foreigner in our schools demands that he be taught to communicate in English with English speaking people because this is his most vital need, and as a basis for the later understanding of the printed and written thoughts of others.

This definition of purpose reduced to school room practice is quite generally accepted by teachers of adult foreigners. Leaving out of consideration the problem of teaching English speaking adults whether of foreign or of native birth, teachers are agreed that the three school exercises—speaking—reading—writing—are relatively important in the teaching of English and relatively worth while to the non-English speaking pupil in the order named. To the foreigner learning a second language to be used as medium of communication and not for the training to be derived from the process of learning, spoken language is more vital than printed or written and a reading knowledge of the language is more likely to be used than is the ability to write it. It need hardly be pointed out that this principle need not

3

exclude the teaching of reading and writing from the very beginning as a means of forming multiple associations with language forms to be used in speaking. On the contrary, the three kinds of exercises are intimately related but the relative stress in the selection of subject matter and in the time to be given to each exercise may be determined by the application of the principle.

DIRECT METHODS

Our procedure in teaching depends on the content of the pupils' minds. Children come to us with minds stocked with concepts, with their control of language far behind their control of things. The adult foreigner, on the other hand, has a word for most objects in his environment. Moreover, he can, within the limits of his education, express himself more or less clearly, forcibly and beautifully. An object calls for a word both from the child and from the adult. Their response will, however, be different. The English speaking child will say "pencil," the German "Bleistift," the Frenchman "crayon." The problem for the teacher of immigrants is to have the foreigner associate the object "pencil" with the word "pencil," rather than with the word "crayon" or "Bleistift." It is more economical to make the short cut from the percept "pencil" to the word "pencil" than it is to form a three-fold association of percept "pencil"—word "crayon"—word "pencil." This is an illustration of the pedagogic dictum that one doesn't know a language until one has learned to think in it. Thinking here consists in short-circuiting the current from percept to motor accomplishment in pronouncing the word.

Although this short-circuiting process is the desideratum in all foreign language instruction, it is very difficult to obtain because of certain fundamental laws of human nature. Among them the law of habit has so strengthened the native associations that "Returning were as tedious as go o'er." Hence the hesitation, picking and choosing of words that one notices in listening to the English of the foreigner.

Thinking is always more difficult than memorizing. Pupils will readily understand and accept as a general principle that a language must be learned in use. It is difficult, however, to rid the individual mind of the obsession that the law does not apply in this one case that "my" difficulty is unique, and that "I" learn a language best when the word is translated. This is one of the psychological reasons which explain the pupil's desire for a teacher who speaks his own language. Foreigners will also prefer a text-book containing lists of words translated into their native tongues. The more educated pupils very frequently bring a dictionary to school, and one may see them digging up definitions and translations of unfamiliar words in the course of a lesson. Yet the teacher who translates, the book with the vocabularies and the dictionary are retarding forces, in the earliest lessons at least, in the process of acquiring English because they repeat the double association of percept—foreign word English word.

4

The dictionary and the vocabulary do serve a very useful purpose after the pupil has acquired enough conversational English to need new symbols to express ideas and sentences which he already knows how to form, but in the earliest stages, progress will be most rapid if all association be made direct.

The term, direct method, therefore, serves to explain only one element—an important one—in the teaching of English, i.e., the use by the teacher of the English language in teaching English. Most teachers of immigrants use some form of direct method in their English classes, but the term *direct* does not describe all of their procedure nor even the most characteristic part of it. Some other basis than the language used must be found for classifying the methods employed in teaching language and such a basis is found in the process of learning or in the unit of advance in teaching. On this basis we have

1—Synthetic methods
2—Analytic methods
3—Analytic-synthetic methods.

SYNTHETIC METHODS

A method by which a teacher plans to "build" up a knowledge of the language by the process of accretion beginning with the elements and proceeding to larger units is called Snythetic. All such methods whether based on letters, phonic combinations, syllables, words or sentences serve to illustrate what Prof. Sweet calls the Arithmetical Fallacy, i.e., that in teaching language, the sum of all the parts do not equal the whole. Teachers sometimes seek to justify the use of a purely synthetic method by quoting a much misunderstood pedagogic maxim "From the simple to the complex." Anything is simple, however, not because it is logically simple, but because of its interest and meaning. Thus the expression, "Have you a job for me?" is simpler and easier to teach than any one word in the sentence. The metaphor "building a vocabulary" is derived from the process of building objects in the physical world where by adding one element to another, an edifice is finally erected. Language, however, is more like an organism, it grows and develops by use rather than by being set together like the parts of a machine.

Frequently, attempts have been made to standardize the teaching of English on an efficiency basis, using the methods of quantity production for which American shops are justly famous. Such attempts must prove abortive because the unit in language teaching is not a fixed standard unit.

1—THE ALPHABET AS THE UNIT

In teaching English speaking children to read, modern teachers no longer begin by teaching the alphabet and then proceeding to phonograms, words and finally to sentences. Teaching a new language is a much more difficult process than teaching to read a language familiar to the learner, less dependent on the recognition of symbols or on the combination of sounds produced by uttering the sound called forth by symbols. Few teachers today would attempt to instruct foreigners in using English as a means of communicating their thought by teaching the letters of the alphabet. The following excerpt from an outline of method published by a well known industrial organization is an example of a reversion to a pedagogy long since discarded by schools and recently re-discovered in the attempt to hurry the process of Americanization.

"The alphabet is the basis of the English language, and should be used in forming the words of the beginner's vocabulary. A thorough drill should be given to the sounding of the letters a, e, i, o, u, w and y, and the division clearly shown between vowel and consonant letters. The .order of work in building up a simple usable vocabulary should be nouns, pronouns, adjectives, verbs, adverbs, prepositions, etc."

"Write the alphabet on the blackboard—both capital and small letters. Explain to the pupils through the interpreter, that, as the alphabet is the basis of the language, they must learn it first in order to build up words for their vocabulary. Give a twenty minute drill on sounding and learning the form of the letters. Have individual pupils point out the letters and sound them. Group the letters as to form such as loop letters b, f, h, j, k, l, y, etc. Use other methods to fix the form and sound of the letter in the mind of the pupil.

"Build up words for the vocabulary through the objective method beginning with the thing the pupil is most interested in himself. Explain through the interpreter that they must name the object pointed to in their own language first, then give them the name of the object in English. The teacher points to a pupil's ear, the class sounds the name of the object in their own language, the teacher sounds it in English, pupils repeat it after him until well sounded. Teacher and pupils then build the word from the alphabet by the following method."

"The teacher points to the letter "e" in the alphabet, the pupils sound it. The teacher brings down the letter "e" on the blackboard, the pupils again sound it. Use the same method with a and r until the word ear is built up. Build up eye, nose, hair, face, etc."

"Drill and review are very essential in this work. When the pupils have acquired a vocabulary of fifty nouns, pronouns and adjectives may then be introduced—using them in connection with nouns already taught. Later on introduce verbs, then adverbs—using them in connection with nouns and pronouns already taught to form complete 'sentences."

2—THE WORD AS THE UNIT

The meaning of an isolated word may be clear to the learner and yet he may find difficulty in using it. The so-called classical methods —in teaching Latin and Greek—is a striking example of this truth.

For the teacher a list of words which the pupils are likely to recognize in their daily needs would have great value. Such lists cannot be standardized because they depend on a host of variable factors such as occupations, physical environment, culture, education, opportunities for using of English. The danger to be avoided in promulgating lists of words is that they will be taught as single words and not as a basis for coherent language.

When single words are the unit of instruction, the prevailing method of teaching is that used by teachers of other modern languages in explaining the meaning of nouns. Thus, the teacher points to a desk and says, "This is a desk." In a highly inflected language like French or German, the procedure has some justification, because the teacher's problem is to insure correctness by associating in the pupil's mind the correct article denoting person, number, gender, or case. Thus, the teacher of French repeats, "Que est-ce que c'est?" because the pupil must be drilled to repeat "C'est *la* bouche," and C'est *le* nez." The teacher of German asks, "Wass ist das?" because the pupil must be taught to say, "Das ist *der* Kopf", *die* Nase, *das* Aug."

In teaching English, however, with its simple rule of gender and its uninflected nouns, this procedure is meaningless and wasteful. The method does not serve the purpose for which teachers of other modern languages use it, nor does it serve the purpose of teaching the meanings of the words intended to be taught. As a result of the frequent repetition of "This is," "That is," "These are," "Those are," the pupil does indeed learn to speak these comparatively unimportant sentences, but he does not learn the meanings of the nouns that follow, except by accident. The meanings of the words intended to be taught, drop out of the "apperceptive mass" of the pupil as fast as their meanings are made clear; they are rarely acquired by him, because he cannot use them, except in a formal way, in answer to such a question as the teacher has asked. The consequent failure to drill the word to be taught through a variety of associations in use, makes it difficult for the pupil even to remember the meaning of the word, to say nothing of using it in an original way to convey a meaning. In some of the older texts, exercises like the following are found:

This is a book	This is a pen
This is a chair	This is a pencil
Is this a book?	Is this a paper?
Is this a pen?	Is this a table?

Is that a collar?
   No, that is not a collar; that is a tie.
Is that a vest?
   Yes, that is a vest.
Is that a glove?
   No, that is not a glove, that is a handkerchief.

The synthetic process, using isolated words as the unit of advance, cannot be generally employed to build a vocabulary, but it is valuable as an occasional device to make the meaning of a new term clear by objectifying it. The distinction between building up a vocabulary in preparation for future use by the "This is," "That is," process and teaching the meaning of the word by associating it with an object, is the distinction between a method and a device. As a method it fails, when used consistently, to do the work for which it was intended; i.e. to build a vocabulary; as a device, it succeeds in clarifying meanings. As a method, it is useless; as a device, it is valuable. The best way to teach the meaning of the word "ceiling," is to point to it and not to talk about it. But to continue the process by naming the objects in the classroom, the parts of the body, the occupations of the pupils, is a method for building a catalogue rather than a vocabulary.

3—CLASSICAL OR GRAMMATICAL SYNTHESIS

The content of grammar has recently undergone a shrinking process, as a result of a clearer definition of its purpose and of its value in helping the pupil to speak, read, and write, English. In teaching English to English speaking pupils, grammar is taught for some of the following reasons: first, to understand difficult passages, by understanding syntactical relationships; second, to establish principles for the resolution of a doubt, e. g., "I know it to be she", or "her"; third, to impart a body of scientific knowledge of the tools of language; fourth, to furnish a medium for elementary logical training.

No illusions are entertained that grammar helps in understanding meanings that are not otherwise understandable or that grammar helps the pupil, except in rare instances, to use English more effectively as a medium of communication. Teachers rather rely on habit forming exercises than on formal conjugations and declensions to impress correct English idiom on their pupils.

Educated non-English speaking adults, however, frequently desire instruction in English grammar because they know that in other European languages, correctness of expression depends largely on a grammatical knowledge of inflections. Teachers have, therefore, sought to satisfy this natural craving for correctness by organizing their instruction on a grammatical instead of on a psychological basis without realizing that, in comparison with other languages, English is a grammarless tongue. This accounts for the dispute whether English instruction should begin with nouns or verbs; it results in teaching principal parts of verbs to pupils who cannot use any part in sentences and in exhausting the possibilities of a verb by conjugating it in all persons and numbers. The fundamental error in all such instruction is, that the teacher is thinking of the subject matter and not of the pupil and of the latter's needs for expression. Certainly at the beginning little is to be gained by spending time on conjugations. The knowledge so acquired is useless for some time to come. The pupils cannot go into the street or into the shop and say,

I	I walk	go
my or mine	Thou walkest	went
me	he walks	going
you	we walk	gone
our or ours	you walk	
us	they walk	

and when the time comes to use the correct word, he finds it imbedded in a series into which he must dig, ere it comes to his mind.

However, after the learner has habituated himself to use correct forms, it is desirable to present a schematic outline of the difficulties that the pupil has mastered. Beyond such grammatical exercises, it is doubtful whether grammar functions in the discourse of non-English speaking pupils, and surely not when taught to beginners, is it to be relied upon to build for the future.

ANALYTIC METHODS

A language method is analytic when, in the process of teaching, a comparatively large unit such as a sentence or a series of sentences is broken up into smaller units, such as phrases, words, syllables or letters. Such methods in teaching are based on the psychological principle "that the mind works from the undefined whole to the parts."

Thus, we take in an entire building without necessarily knowing the number of bricks used in constructing it; we know people without necessarily knowing the color of their eyes, and we read words without necessarily being able to spell them. Our first perceptions are always vague, and are concerned with totalities, rather than with their component elements. Only later do these elements interest us, when they are needed as instruments for the better understanding of the larger units in which they are found. To a foreigner learning English, a sentence is more valuable than a single word, and a word more valuable than a letter. Analytic processes of teaching, therefore, besides conforming to the psychology of learning, also furnish the pupil with such a content as is most valuable to him.

1. GOUIN OR THEME METHOD

As a bare principle, the proposition that isolated words and unrelated subject matter is difficult to teach and more difficult to retain needed no scientific or empirical proof. It was not until the 1880's however, that the principle was applied in the teaching of modern languages and then largely through the psychological analysis of Francois Gouin.

After trying a variety of the then known "methods"—translation, the dictionary, conjugation, grammatical—he arrived at the following axiomatic conclusions:

1. That speaking knowledge of a language is primarily learned through the ear.
2. That learning isolated words—nouns—verbs—does not enable the student to put them together in speech.
3. That the best method of teaching a person to speak is to furnish exercise in the classroom in speaking exactly what he wants to say outside of the classroom.
4. That to insure the ability to understand and to use ordinary words as a second language, it is necessary to associate them with other words in a variety of ways in a series of sentences.
5. That oral speech precedes written and therefore ability to read or write a language is predicated upon ability to understand meanings.
6. That in teaching a person to speak a second language, a beginning must be made with oral language, not only because oral language is the basis for visible language, but because to reverse the process by beginning with visible language is to cause confusion in pronunciation.

Gouin watched a number of little children playing a game in which incidentally they learned the meanings of expressions in association with the acts which they performed much the same as foreign children in America might learn the meanings of the English sentences in playing the game "This is the way I wash my clothes," "This is the way I iron my clothes."

From this germ, Gouin developed the "theme" on the idea of constructing a series of sentences on a single topic and associating verbal expression with the performance of the act.

Gouin defines a theme as "A general act defined by a series of particular acts. Considered from another point of view, that of logic, this exercise represents:

1. A general end, unique and simple (to open the door).
2. A group, a series of means conducive to this end."

Thus the teacher determines the end "to open the door." She then constructs a number of simple sentences describing the actions necessary for opening the door. In these sentences it is the verbs that play the principal parts. "The verb is the living center around which in the phrase, gravitate all the nouns, whether subject or complement, with all their train of prepositions and adjectives." In attaining the end—to open the door—teacher and pupils perform the necessary actions which are the means, i.e., they walk, get to the door, stop, stretch out, take hold of, turn, push, etc. As each action is performed, it is accompanied by the appropriate descriptive sentence. The teacher at the same time shows her approval of intelligence and understanding. The sentences in the first themes bear to each other the relation of succession, but later they may bear such other relationships as those of cause and effect, the whole and

10

its parts. The development of a theme is not complete until the sentences are written on the board and the verbs placed to the right for emphasis. Thus the first theme "to open the door" will appear on the board like this:

I walk towards the door.................I walk
I get to the door........................I get to
I stop at the door.......................I stop
I stretch out my hand....................I stretch out
I take hold of the knob..................I take hold
I turn the knob.........................I turn
I push the door ....I push
The door moves ....moves
The door turns on its hinges.............turns
I let go the knob.......................I let go

Now the pupils are ready to read from the blackboard. The teacher insures understanding by requiring pupils to repeat the action as the sentence is read.

The sentences as developed illustrate what Gouin calls "objective language." He makes a point of having the teacher approve the efforts of the pupils as they act and give the sentences. These ejaculations called "subjective language" have a two-fold function. They add to the pupil's vocabulary and they serve to speed him on. The following examples of subjective language are taken from the New York City syllabus:

"Good. Right. Wrong. Very good. Yes. No. That's good. That's right. No, no, that is not right. Try again. Thank you. You are a good boy. Is that right? Do you think so? I like that. I am glad. That is fine. That was well done. I am glad you remember. You could not do better. I am pleased with you. Do your best, etc."

The following are the steps in the treatment of a theme:

1. An end proposed—the subject of the theme.

In the selection of *ends* or theme topics, the teacher is guided by the consideration that the content of the theme must be valuable to the pupils under instruction; a theme on "riveting a boiler" will not be useful to a group of tailors, and a theme on "washing the baby" will not be valuable to a group of maiden seamstresses.

2. A number of short sentences describing the means to attain the end.

The sentences must be short and simple so that only one idea may be presented at a time. Thus the sentence, "I open the door" may be demonstrated by action and the pupil can understand the words to describe only one act, since only one act was performed. Were the sentence compound or complex, the

11

wrong association might be made, e.g., "I open the door when you knock." It is possible for the pupil to be confused as to which words describe "opening" and which "knocking."

3. "One sole relationship, always the same from one end of the exercise to the other, that of succession in time, enjoys to the exclusion of all others, the privilege of connecting the end with the means."

The sentences must, therefore, not only be unified by the topic, relate to it strictly on the principle of unity, but they must be coherent, related to each other, growing out of each other. To secure this coherence between the sentences of the theme, Gouin insists that the words "and then" be understood after each sentence to provide a succession in time. This device is an aid to the teacher in constructing a theme and a help to the pupil in recalling the sentence. The principle of coherence is vital to the organization of lessons on the theme plan. It insures connected sentences, which as was pointed out are more easily remembered than isolated sentences or words; each sentence helps to recall the other sentences in the theme series much the same way as one line of poetry helps to recall the next line. A double association is thus provided by the process of theme development—1—An association of the words with the act; 2—An association of the words with the other sentences in the theme.

4. Emphasis on the verb which must be one frequently used in the experience of the learner. "The various moments of the action are distinguished with care and separated one from another by a sign or guiding mark, in order to assure a logical exposition and an easy assimilation."

The verb is frequently placed to the right or to the left of each sentence to emphasize the fact that the action is carried by the words.

5. Oral development in which the pupil sees, does, hears, understands, speaks, reads.

The complete development of the theme is as follows:

1st. The teacher performs the act and speaks the sentence; e.g., "I open my eyes." The first appeal is, therefore, through the ear and the association established is directly between expression and idea.

2nd. Pupils perform the act and speak the sentence. This supplies a supplementary association between the idea and the spoken words of the pupil.

3rd. The teacher performs the act, speaks the sentence and writes or points the words on the board. Some teachers permit pupils to read these sentences as developed in a text. This gives another form of association-idea-spoken-words-written words.

12

4th. Pupils perform the act, speak the sentence, read it from the board. Again a triple association.

5th. Pupils copy the sentence.

6th. Pupils write the sentence from dictation.

7th. Pupils write the sentence from memory.

8th. The teacher approves the efforts of the pupils at all stages by encouraging him in such words as "Good", "That's right", "Try again", "I like that".

It is customary to begin with the theme "to open the door" because every room has a door and because the sentences in the theme lend themselves so easily to the method. Teachers who understand home, industrial and racial influences, exercise considerable ingenuity in selecting and constructing themes. Their value to the pupil depends upon their availability for immediate use in the conversation for which the pupil has a need. Whatever of idealism our immigrants are contributing to America does not appear in their first lessons in English. Then they are pragmatists. They are perhaps too polite to ask "of what use is this to me" when a teacher introduces sentences which have no bearing on present use, but they very quickly show their disapproval, and the teacher who neglects sentences of value today for sentences that may be of value five years from now, will tomorrow find himself without a class.

Age, sex, occupation, education and many other factors in the environment determine what special vocabulary will be of greatest utilitarian value. With these determining influences, the successful teacher of English to foreigners must make himself familiar. He must overcome the reticence of his pupils by showing a personal interest in their welfare, an interest which may at times amount almost to prying into their affairs. Some activities are universal, and these form the basis of the following suggestive list of themes:

To go to work	To look for rooms	To go to the library
To wash myself	To pay rent	To send money home
To bathe	To buy groceries	To introduce a friend
To eat breakfast	To go to the doctor	To telephone
To make the fire	To go to school	To cook dinner
To go to a restaurant	To write a letter	To deposit money
To look for work	To register a letter	To draw money
To take the train	To visit (the Museum)	To spend a holiday
To go home	To clean the house	

The value of the theme method lies in its naturalness and organization. Its definite function is to give the pupils the English idiom and a vocabulary in a context. The words will otherwise be unintelligible without the intermediation of his native symbols for the ideas expressed. As in all organized work, the pupil is by this method given a natural aid by which to remember; each sentence recalls its

13

associated idea which leads to the next idea with its associated expression. By the method of development, which is a part of the theme method, we overcome, to some extent, the trouble foreigners have in pronouncing difficult words. It was pointed out that oral development always precedes the writing of words and sentences. Hence, when the pupil hears the teacher pronounce such words as "tough," "though," "girl," "friend," etc., he imitates the sound produced by the teacher without being conscious of the spelling. In matters of pronunciation, confusion arises when pupils are permitted to see the word before they know how to pronounce it by the process of imitation.

The Gouin method has a definite place in the teaching of English, but it is not the whole of method. "Methods must be supplementary, not competitive." With beginning pupils, the procedure so far outlined is highly successful, but it soon outlives its usefulness. With it there can be little variety in structure; the first person singular, pleasant as it may be when speaking of actions which command the admiration and applause of our co-workers, becomes painfully shrunk when used in connection with "washing the teeth," and "putting on the pants."

By way of summary, the Gouin method is sound when it insists, 1st, that language is best taught through a content couched in unified coherent serial language; 2nd, that sentences of this content must be understandable by the pupil by direct association through objectification or dramatization; 3rd, that sentences be short to prevent confusion; 4th, that themes be short to aid in memorising.

In the development of his method, however, perhaps because he was laid under the necessity of expanding his thought into a universal method, Gouin lost sight of his principles and made a fetich of the form. Emerson says, "Each prophet comes presently to identify himself with his thought and to esteem his hat and shoes sacred." Gouin as well as many of his adapters seem to lose sight of the functions of the method and to rely on the magical potency of some incidental and minor attributes of the procedure. Gouin becomes mystical and metaphysical in his later chapters especially when he tries to apply the method to the teaching of literature to non-English speaking students by the process of cutting up the lines and placing a word to the right.

It is not surprising that Gouin's followers, many of whom saw in his method only an artificial arrangement of sentences, should have seized upon this characteristic to teach English by arranging the sentences of a paragraph vers libre fashion. As an example of such abuse of Gouin's principles the following lesson from Montgomery's Talking English is quoted:

The Ship of the Desert

1. The camel is important in desert journeys	camel
2. where the heat is overpowering,	heat
3. and the mercury registers 120 degrees,	mercury

14

4. He has extra stomachs as separate reservoirs.	extra
5. These can contain large supplies of water.	contain
6. Camels are employed in cold sections also.	employed
7. On roads where snow has been packed hard,	packed
8. their bare feet are liable to slip and spread.	liable
9. To prevent this their owners cut grooves	cut
10. in the tough soles of their feet.	soles
11. A camel looming up out of a dense fog	looming
12. is a terrifying sight to travelers,	sight
13. especially if heading a string of companions.	heading
14. His immense size and proportionate strength	size
15. make him valuable property to possess.	valuable
16. When he swallows the dough ball fed to him,	swallows
17. you can watch it slide down his throat.	watch

It is apparent that no good pedagogic reason exists for such an arrangement of sentences and it can only give an inexperienced teacher the belief that somehow this artificiality makes English instruction easy. These sentences cannot be dramatized; if they can be understood without dramatization there is no need for the form of a theme. The placing of words to the right, the chopping up of an otherwise perfectly good paragraph is hocus pocus. The sentences are not coherent; a pupil who forgets what the second sentence is, is not helped to remember it by going back to the first sentence.

ANALYTIC-SYNTHETIC METHODS

An analytic synthetic process of teaching is eclectic. It utilizes the analytic features beginning with large units which it then proceeds to re-arrange for the construction of new units of language. In a purely analytic process of teaching a pupil is left with sentences and with expressions without training in shifting them around to meet new situations.

The necessity for breaking up a series of sentences into new permutations and combinations forces teachers to adapt other supplementary procedures.

1. The Frankfort Variation

An interesting modification of the Gouin method was developed in the schools of Frankfort. The variation consists in basing sentences on "things seen" rather than on "things done," thus permitting great variety in person, number and tense. For example, the teacher steps to his desk, takes a piece of chalk and writes on the board. The pupils describe the actions of the teacher by saying "you are going to your desk," "you are taking a piece of chalk," "you are writing on the board," "you put the chalk on the desk," "you erase the writing on the board." A pupil is then called upon to perform the actions of the teacher, while the class or another pupil says "he is walking to the desk," etc. The pupil who performs the action speaks in the first person, while the actions are going on, other pupils speak 'to him and of him in the second and third persons. The tense is varied in a similar manner.

The possibilities for changing person, number and gender and in English particularly for the teaching the progressive form of the verb have made this addition to the pure Gouin method valuable. The variation is possible however only after the pupils have learned the sentences of a number of themes and is applicable only to sentences learned through the themes.

2. Question-Answer Methods

Entirely apart from themes, an analytic-synthetic process of teaching has developed in the use of text-books by means of questions by the teacher and answers by the pupils. The method assumes that pupils have been taught the meaning of the context and proceeds to make use of that context for developing the ability to construct with it sentences and even larger units of expression.

More recent texts divide the subject matter of the lessons into two parts, the first consisting of reading material, the second of questions based on the texts. These questions must be just as carefully graded as the text because they have specific functions in the teaching of English. At first they direct attention to words and phrases in sentences and provide a motivated reason for reading and re-reading the lessons in the book. For example: the students may know the meaning of the sentence "The man drinks water from a glass;" without having a clear concept of any single word in the sentence. The teacher may turn the searchlight of the pupil's mind to any part of the sentence by a proper question at the same time securing repetition with attention. These questions bring in subjects, predicates, complements, or modifying elements. Thus, the teacher, at intervals recurs to the same sentence by the following questions:

"Who drinks water?"

"What does the man do?"

"From what does the man drink water?"

"What does the man drink?"

This necessitates attention to, and repetition of the elements which the pupil is compelled to use in a sentence; in this process he is aided at the beginning by the printed page before him and sometimes by elliptical sentences which he must fill in; e.g.

"The man ———— water from a glass."

"The ———— drinks water from a glass," etc.

Pupils need not, however, be held by such leading strings very long.

For more advanced pupils at least two other grades of questions to accomplish this are possible; first, requiring the pupil to answer in the sentences of the text but not in the order in which the text is written; second, requiring pupils to answer in their own words—to think and talk at the same time.

16

3. The Method of Conversation

The chief function, however, of teaching English to foreigners is to enable the learner to speak in such terms as he will need in making his way in an English speaking community. Set lessons on themes while necessary as a basis for progressive mastery of the language must be supplemented by a content which is conversational and applicable to the daily needs of immigrants who may be expected to learn English in the classroom. Foreigners who voluntarily attend such classes must be given at the very outset a feeling of power that they have acquired the ability to say something to an English speaking person, even though it be but a single English sentence. Basing English instruction on the pupil's extra school life is the surest guarantee that the learner will continue to interest and exert himself in mastering difficulties which otherwise are academic.

The greatest difficulty in teaching English to foreigners is to know how to begin. Picture the situation as seen in a typical classroom. From thirty to fifty men or women are assembled. When the class has been "graded" and is fairly homogeneous as to nationality, age and culture, the problem is simplified. Frequently, however, the size of the school does not permit any classification and the teacher is confronted by a class representing as many as ten nationalities of both sexes ranging in age from sixteen to sixty and comprising illiterates who are experiencing their first lesson in any classroom. Seated by the latter may be graduates of the University of Heidelberg and of Paris, men who can deliver lectures on Kant and on the philosophy of history in their native tongues. The task confronting the experienced teacher under these conditions is enough to try all his powers of control, to bring to bear all his knowledge, his tact and his humanity in the solution of his problem. The inexperienced teacher will be hopelessly confused and will recognize the littleness of his power and the futility of his efforts unless he has an unusual amount of complacency.

It is the duty therefore of supervisors to provide a "set of organized procedures" to overcome the difficulties of the introductory lessons. Briefly, the procedure is as follows: From a list the teacher calls the name of a pupil—"John Smith." If John Smith recognizes his name, the teacher says "stand." As she gives the order, the teacher rises. Each name thus called is followed by the order to stand. The teacher approves the pupils' understanding by such remarks as "good," "fine," "you understand," "that's good," showing at the same time by gesture and by facial expression that she means what she says. In the same way the teacher directs each pupil to sit.

Another way of beginning, valuable where the teacher has no list of pupils from which to call the roll, is to point to himself and say "My name is Frank Brown." Then, pointing to a pupil, he says: "What is your name?" The pupil is expected to answer, "My name

17

is John Smith." If the pupil does not understand, the teacher calls other pupils until the desired response is obtained. When the class has learned the meaning of "My name is———," they are taught to say "Your name is ———" "What is my name " "What is your name?" etc. The sentences are usually written on the blackboard and are copied by pupils.

By this means in a purely supplementary way and entirely apart from the coherent theme and text-book lessons, the pupil is furnished with a number of idiomatic expressions. For example, no matter what else is taught, it is worth teaching such expressions as

> "My name is ———
> "I live at ———
> "I am a ——— (carpenter)
> "I work for Mr. ———
> "I have a job."
> "How do you do?"
> "I am very well."
> "I am sick."
> "My head aches."
> "I have a pain in my chest."
> "I am married."
> "I am single."
> "How much does this hat cost?"
> "What time is it?"
> "It is half past eight."
> The names of relatives.

In practice such conversational exercises precede set lessons and are largely individual. Pupils are encouraged to come early when they realize that they may spend a few minutes in personal conversation with the teacher.

The theme will furnish the later topics of conversation. Adults, especially those from Southern Europe, will very early attempt original voluble discussions, provided the teacher has stimulated the desire to communicate and has not used the conversation period for a monologue. The pupils must be encouraged by questions, by suggestions, by helping with a word; their conversation must not be discouraged by petty criticism of pronunciation, of grammar or of vocabulary. There will be a time for all this. The conversation lesson is full of suggestion for the teacher; words that need drill on pronunciation; foreign idioms to be replaced by English; drill on agreement of subject, predicate, etc. For each of these, there should be a specific time. All drill on form should grow out of the content. The conversation furnishes the content. The exercise in phonics, grammar, spelling, etc., are form.

A natural flow of conversation is sometimes difficult to secure because of the unnatural and formal conditions in the schoolroom. At home or among his friends, a man talks "with" the people in the room rather than "at" some one who is the center of attraction. The more nearly school conditions approximate life conditions, the more sprightly will the conversation be and the better will the teaching be. There will also be more opportunities for the pupil to make mistakes, but teachers should hardly complain of that. Like the doctor, they should rather gloat over the "beautiful case" of queer English which it is their privilege to "cure."

As a step toward securing natural conditions, it is suggested that conversations be based on topics of vital interest. In the earliest stages, these topics will be found in the themes, which, as has been shown, are themselves to be gauged by the yard stick of utility and of interest.

But admirable as the theme and the other exercises are, they fail to give the pupil what he most needs at once—the ability to use idiomatic English in his daily intercourse with English-speaking strangers. The complaint is frequently heard from high school and college graduates that after years of study in French or in German, they are unable to order a meal, to buy a hat, or to ask one's way in the streets of Paris or Berlin without resorting to English. The high schools and colleges do not pretend to teach this bread and butter conversation. They refuse to be so basely utilitarian. They are actuated by a series of mixed motives in which culture, and the ability to appreciate the literature in a foreign language vie with correctness of pronunciation and idiomatic use. The teacher of English to foreigners in the United States must suffer from no such mental astigmatism. The immigrant requires no preparation for life; he is in the midst of life and demands rather immediate adjustment. He seeks to be compensated for his sacrifice in coming to school by acquiring the immediate ability to say the thing that he must say in English. He is impatient of results and is distrustful of promises of potential ability. He cares nothing for culture. He is perfectly content for the present at least, to think in his own tongue,

> I walk to the store.
> I open the door.
> I see the clerk.
> The clerk shows me a suit.

provided that when he gets there, he is able to say:

> This suit does not fit.
> It is too dear.
> Have you nothing cheaper?

Skill to say a few necessary things rather than ability to comprehend a great many is what the foreigner needs. It must be clearly understood that what is taught in the theme and in the reading lesson serves a very valuable purpose if it teaches the pupil to understand English. But it is not merely understanding that the foreigner must be taught; far more important for him is it to acquire the ability to communicate his ideas. The teacher, therefore, now emphasises those sentences which the foreigner will be called upon to use in his intercourse with English-speaking people and he neglects those sentences which the foreigner need not necessarily know how to say. Since teaching a person how to acquire skill in speaking is more difficult than teaching him how to understand, it becomes important to limit the number of sentences to those that are needed at once. To impart such skill, locutions must be specifically based on the probable activities in which the foreigner will engage. Unless these idiomatic expressions are taught, the foreigner will translate his own idiom and produce the tortured sentences and monstrosities frequently heard on the vaudeville stage.

For teaching these everyday expressions the method of dramatization is most successfully used. To illustrate: two pupils are instructed to take the parts of salesman and of customer. As the dialogue proceeds the teacher asks other pupils to express the same thoughts in better English, at the same time writing the correct expressions on the board. After other pupils have gone through the same exercise, the class is instructed to copy those expressions which they like best. After a ten minutes' lesson of this kind on "How to find one's way," the following conversation was carried on between a man and woman immigrant:

Woman—I beg your pardon, can you tell me where the nearest subway entrance is?

Man (removing his hat as soon as spoken to)—Yes, ma'am. Walk two blocks north (pointing north), and you will see it.

Woman—Thank you (bowing).

Man—You're quite welcome.

Other pupils who went through the same procedure used other English expressions which they found on the board, e.g., excuse me—would you mind telling me—permit me to show you—not at all. Such expressions require emphasis in the teaching process, if only to give the foreigner confidence that he is able to make himself understood. It is not intended that dramatization be the entire method, nor is it intended to supersede other methods or other exercises which a teacher of English finds valuable. But these dramatizations provide exercises for which none others are as well adapted. The following topics suggest conversations of a practical nature from which a teacher may select those which are most needed by his pupils:

Buying—a railroad ticket—a hat—shoes—cigars—suit—furniture on the installment plan.

Repairing—shoes—clothing—machinery—furniture.

Renting—a flat—a room at a boarding house or hotel.

Ordering—a meal—an expressman.

Checking a trunk.

Asking—one's way—in street—in car—in department store—at
  a railroad terminal.
Telling time.
Applying for—position—raise in salary—day off.
Getting a license—to peddle—to sell liquors—to marry.
Sending money home.
Ordering insurance policy—fire—life—accident.
Opening bank account.
Introducing a friend.
Seeing a friend off.
Inviting someone to call—to dinner—theatre—to visit.

INCIDENTAL DEVICES

At all times it is necessary to vitalize the lesson by varying the
procedure by securing vividness and spontaneity. The following are
devices which may be used as they are needed. They should not,
however, be repeated so frequently that they frustrate the purpose for
which they are intended.

1. The teacher points to a book and says "this is a book."
   Teacher: "What is this?" Pupil: "This is a book." So
   with the parts of the body, clothing, money, days of the
   week, etc., wherever possible, the teacher has the object
   present, points to it and gives its name.

2. Obeying commands, e.g., "put your hands on the desk." The
   pupil performs the act and says "I put my hands on my desk."

3. Question—answer, e.g., "what is the chair made of?" "It is
   made of wood."

4. Reading and acting, e.g., pupil reads "open the door" and
   performs the action.

5. Labeling, e. g., a card with the word "chair" written on it
   is given to a pupil with directions to place it where it belongs.

6. Filling in context, e.g., today is ——. What day was yesterday. Tomorrow will be ——? It is — o'clock.

7. Pantomime or dramatization—a method valuable for giving
   the meaning of verbs easily illustrated by actions, e.g., he
   sawed the board—the child stumbled—he turned and fled.

8. Reading aloud by the teacher accompanied by gesture, expression and play of features, e. g., "The haughty nobleman
   spoke in a thin squeaky voice." By assuming an attitude of
   haughtiness and by using the voice, the teacher helps pupils
   to understand the meanings of descriptive terms.

9. By means of "Mediate perception, i.e., pictures. This method
   has not been used to any great extent in this country,
   perhaps not without reason. In Germany, however, it is
   very fully developed, so much so that beautifully colored charts,

21

such as the Hölzl Wandtafel, are specially prepared to meet the needs of the pupils learning English and French. The pictures portray scenes from urban and country life. The pupils name the objects seen, describe and talk about them. Properly used, the method has great value. We need hardly go to the trouble of preparing elaborately colored charts when text-book writers have followed the method of the Orbis Pictus of Comenius. Newspapers, magazines and other supplementary material add a vast amount of pictures suitable for this purpose. Mons. Berlitz sounds a note of warning against relying too much on interpreting pictures. "Who would know at the sight of a cliff overhanging the sea, at the top of which stands a woman with flowing garb and other signs of despair and suicidal intention, that the picture is meant to represent—a sunset?" Having in mind some such criticism, Prof. Jesperson says: "The objection comes from a closet philosopher. There is no danger except for one who would try to learn a language by himself exclusively through pictures." Prof. Sweet bases his objection to the method on the belief that ideas gotten from pictures are vague as compared with ideas obtained by means of translation. Thus, the teacher may point to the window and say, "This is a window," but the pupil may interpret this to mean "This is a pane of glass." To overcome this difficulty, the teacher follows up his first sentence by saying, "There are two windows in the room," and "Open the window."

10. A word or an expression may be explained by using other known elements, so as to make a new word evident through context, e.g., "There are twelve months in the year. The first is called January, the second February, the third March, etc." Here the pupils may gather the meaning of the words months, first, second, etc. A pupil comes across the sentence, "They went to the Capital," and does not know the meaning of Capital. The teacher says "Berlin is the capital of Germany, Petrograd is the capital of Russia, Rome is the capital of Italy," and the pupils will all shake their heads in assured confidence that they understand. Prepositions are best explained by this method. The teacher holds a book "on" the table, "under" the table, "beside" the table, "in front of," "behind," etc., each time expressing the sentence and having the pupils perform the acts and saying the words. The method of definition is a variation from the context method for the purpose of making clear the meanings of words. Simple definitions or synonyms with which the pupils are already familiar may be used to advantage, for example, "A messenger is a person sent on an errand," "A

widow is a woman whose husband has died." The method of defining terms is most easily abused and should therefore be sparingly used. Teachers fall into the habit of giving definitions which are more difficult to understand than the terms defined and, as a test of comprehension, they demand from their scholars definitions of terms which are already in their lowest terms, or else are definable only by synonyms more difficult than the terms to be defined. Thus it is bad practice to give or demand definitions of such words as day, light, bread, darkness. These words may best be understood by using some of the other methods suggested.

READING FROM TEXT

After three or four lessons, the pupils will have completed their first theme and they may then take up the reading of a text-book. This is perhaps the most unsatisfactory of all processes used for the teaching of English to foreigners. The methods used in teaching children to read are hardly applicable to the different conditions which one meets in the teaching of adults. Supervisors are generally agreed that the teaching of reading to children is on a rather low plane as compared with the teaching of other subjects. When we come to the teaching of reading to adults, there is a lack of standard as to what to do or what to expect pupils to do. The result is that the usual reading lesson is a mechanical mispronunciation of words, punctuated by the teacher's impatient correction of errors, followed by calling upon "Next" to read.

The cause of our poor reading lessons is the general failure to understand the psychology of reading. Says Inspector Hughes in his Teaching to Read, "Reading is generally accepted as meaning to read aloud. Much confusion has resulted from this general misconception. Reading is the power of getting thought from visible language. It is the power of recognizing in visible form the language with which the child is already familiar in the spoken form." Here is where method of teaching English-speaking children to read must part company with method of teaching adult foreigners to read. For the foreigner is not familiar in any form with the language which he is called upon to read. He is given a three-fold task: First, to extract thought from language which he does not understand; second, to express the thought; third to pronounce the words. Any one of these feats is enough to engage all his powers at one time.

Reading is badly taught not only when teachers fail to see the relationship of silent reading to oral reading, but when they fail to see the distinction between learning to read and learning language. In learning language, we teach pupils to associate words with objects, ideas or experiences. The language teacher is concerned with having the pupil acquire correct expressions to portray states of mind. In learning to read we teach pupils to associate visible language with lan-

23

guage which they already know. We do not teach children to read before they can speak and we cannot teach adults to read a language in which they do not recognize meanings. High school students may very easily be taught to pronounce Latin words but that does not enable them to read. Adult foreigners may be taught to recognize English words after a fashion but that does not enable them to understand English, to speak English or to write it. It merely teaches them to utter sounds. In order that adults learning English as a second language may be enabled to read it, they must be taught to understand so much of the language as they are being taught to read. A variety of method depending on the text, the progress of the class, etc., are available for this end.

1. In an introduction, the teacher uses the new words and expressions to be found in the selection for reading. These words are developed orally, the meanings made clear and the words written on the blackboard. When the pupil meets the words in the context, he greets them with a flash of recognition.

2. The teacher develops the content by means of questions. "I eat three meals a day. My first meal is in the morning before I go to work. This I call my breakfast. At noon I stop work and eat my dinner. Noon is at 12 o'clock. When I come home from work in the evening I eat my supper." The teacher asks the following questions: How many meals do you eat? What is your first meal? When do you eat your first meal? When do you stop? What meal do you eat at noon? As the answers are given, the important words "meals," "breakfast," "before," "noon," "dinner," etc., are written on the board.

3. A discussion based on a picture will serve to introduce the unknown expressions.

4. Oral reading by the teacher besides serving as a model in pronunciation will sometimes help an understanding, especially when the teacher has mimetic powers.

5. Silent reading by the pupils should usually precede all oral reading. This simplifies the process by eliminating thought expression and reduces the danger of calling or rather miscalling words. Silent reading gives the teacher an opportunity of answering individual questions as to the meaning and pronunciation of simple words or of phrases.

Now the pupils are ready to read aloud. In spite of his foresight in overcoming difficulties, the teacher will still find pupils who miscall words, who phrase improperly, whose accent is faulty and who stumble while they read. The best practice does not permit interruptions while a pupil is reading, because mental processes are interfered with. When a pupil halts he is usually helped over his

24

difficulty in a quiet tone, but corrections are made after the pupil has finished his reading.

If allowed to degenerate into a monotonous calling of words, the reading lesson becomes a splendid soporific and a prime cause for the dwindling in the numbers of the class. Very few of us are such good readers that we give pleasure to those who hear us when we read. Most people prefer to read silently and consider the oral reader a bore. Only in the classroom is he considered a necessity. Natural conditions which prevail outside of the classroom may be approximated by furnishing a reason or a "motive" as pedagogues say, for the oral reading. Place the reader in sole possession of information which the others want and you have established a condition when it becomes necessary to listen to the reader. Hence, oral reading should be resorted to only first, after the pupil has mastered all the technical difficulties of pronunciation and understanding; second, when there is something remarkable about the reading itself, so that it becomes attractive in spite of the familiar content. These conditions presuppose that we furnish an audience for the oral rendition of a selection. The audience is, of course, the class which, after it has heard spoken English for several weeks, will gladly listen to a reader provided the latter has something to say which the others do not know or provided the reader's interpretation is different.

Some of the devices employed by the best teachers of reading in the elementary schools might well be employed by teachers of reading to foreigners.

1. One pupil reads to the class while the others with books closed ask questions for further information, answer questions, obey directions, summarize the reading, or by showing that they could not understand the reader, convince him that he needs further drill on pronunciation and accent.

2. Each pupil selects something from his reader, a newspaper, or a magazine, prepares his reading thoroughly and presents it to the class.

After the reading lesson is over, the pupils show their appreciation and their understanding by means of some of the following devices:

1. Questions on the text proposed by the teacher in the early stages of instruction and by the pupils later on. e.g., the pupil has read, "Mary broke the pitcher." The teacher asks subject, predicate, or complement questions. "Who broke the pitcher?" "What did Mary do with the pitcher?" "What did Mary break?" In each case, the pupils answer in complete sentences, thus learning to ask questions and to give complete statements.

2. Oral reproduction in the pupils' words.

3. Written reproduction by means of dictation or original composition.

25

4. Recasting the sentences by changes in tense, person, number.
5. By means of dramatization or by carrying out the directions.
6. Discussion as to the value or truth of the selection read. This device can only be used when the class has acquired a working vocabulary and facility in expressing thought.
7. Expansions of a single statement into a paragraph by furnishing proof, illustration or examples.
8. By memorizing passages of poetry, proverbs and idiomatic expressions.

PHONICS

Among the purposes for which phonics are employed in teaching English, the following are the most important:

1. To aid in teaching pupils to spell.
2. To train pupils to hear correctly and to make nice distinctions in sound.
3. To correct errors in pronunciation, enunciation, intonation and accent.
4. To aid in learning to read by furnishing a key to the ready recognition of new words.

In the teaching of spelling, phonics are an aid especially in teaching words with a phonetic base. It must be remembered, however, that foreigners have a limited use for spelling and that in English spelling, the syllable rather than the letter is the basis for phonetic grouping.

Teachers of foreigners are inclined to over-emphasize the importance of corrective phonics, especially because accent and foreign idiom disclose foreign birth. In teaching foreign born children, it is undoubtedly worth while spending all needed time to eliminate foreignisms. They may be expected to remain in school long enough to build new habits of speech and their mouth parts are still plastic enough to be affected by continuous effort. The case with adults is entirely different. Their attendance at school is voluntary, uncertain and dependent entirely on their judgment of the worth of the instruction. They regard drill on correct pronunciation as a proper refinement of teachers jealous of the purity of English sounds, of little practical though of great ornamental value. Were it possible to keep adult pupils in school long enough to affect their habits of speech, and were they to consider such a result worth while, it is still questionable whether it could be accomplished. Very seldom is a person who has learned to speak a second language after adolescence able to speak it without foreign accent even though he has an incentive to do so stronger than that which moves most non-English speaking people to be Americanized. Witness the difficulty in this regard of foreign professors of modern languages.

It is worth while, however, to pay some attention to the matter of correctness in pronunciation, if only to present an ideal of the sound of English speech and to point out distinctions in the meanings of words commonly confused by foreigners. The teacher must be able to overcome common defects of speech by pointing out the process of placing the mouth parts. The following chart will help the teacher in directing pupils to pronounce consonants.

| | ORAL | | | NASAL |
Place of articulation	Momentary surd. sonant	Continuous surd. sonant		Continuous sonant
Lips	p b	—	w	m
Lips and teeth....................	— —	th (in) th (y)		—
Tongue and teeth.................	— —	f v		—
Tongue and hard palate (fwd.).....	t d	s z,r		n
Tongue and hard palate (back)....	ch j	sh zh,r		—
Tongue, hard palate, soft palate....	— —	— y,l		—
Tongue and soft palate..........	k g	— —		ng
Various places	h —	— —		—

Besides being able to instruct the pupils in the use of their organs of speech, the teacher ought to be able to suggest a number of helpful devices, e. g.:

Th—soft..............Bite tongue between teeth and blow without sound. Prolong the sound if "d" is produced.

Th—hard.............Same as above, but with sound. If an unvoiced sound is produced, let pupil hum while he is sounding.

W....................Pronounce oo and join with the following sound e. g.,—oo—ait—wait.

Wh..................The sound is pronounced Hw, e. g., hoo—ere, where. If the pupil finds the sound difficult, instruct him to blow and say hoo and ere, or let pupil prepare for whistling and join latter part of the word.

Ng—as in singing.....Prolong the sound by keeping the mouth parts in the same position while pronouncing the sound. Show the difference between king and kink. Feel the breath come out in kink; notice that there is no expulsion of breath in king. Drill on words having this sound of ng.

As a key to recognition of new words, phonics has perhaps greatest value. For this purpose "a phonic element is said to be developed when it has been made a separate object of attention, when it can be recognized and sounded apart from any words, when it can be used in the building and identifying of new words and when, in certain cases, the way to produce it by tongue, lips, or other organs is understood." The first step is easily understood by all foreigners who are not illiterate. They know the sounds of f, m, l, r, s, z, in

27

their own languages and the slight difference between their pronunciation and ours is readily comprehended. Difficulty is experienced with the hard and soft sound of th, with the phonograms like ing, ough, etc. As preparation for analyzing phonic elements, the pupils learn through their themes, object lessons and conversational exercises, a large number of words which they recognize as wholes. The teacher selects some of these words and proceeds as follows: First, she groups them in families, e. g.:

hat	cat	fat
day	pay	lay
wall	tall	fall

The words are then separated into their phonic elements, e.g., h—at. New words are built by prefixing other consonants to the phonic element already learned with the caution that the new words must mean something to the pupil. Second, as soon as the short sounds of a, e, i, o, u, are developed as in the words hat, men, fin, on, suck, the long sounds may be developed as in the words take, theme, fine, loan, tune, by adding silent e to a word, e. g., fin—fine.

In the same way are taught the long sounds of ee, ay, oa as o, ai as a, oo as in wood, oi as in join, aw as in draw, the sounds of ing and ink, is as in girl, u as in burn, ough as in bought, ight as in bright, eigh as in weigh.

In the process of combining or blending phonic elements, the pupils should at once be taught to pronounce each element in a whisper and later to think the sound of each phonogram before attempting the word. Words which do not lend themselves to phonic treatment may sometimes be grouped to form families, and in this way to reinforce each other, e. g., wood—should; where—there; who—whose—whom; these—that—this—those. There will still be a large number of words like dozen, been, once, etc., which do not come under any class but stand out by themselves. These must be taught as sight words and especially taught as such both as to spelling and pronunciation. A five-minute drill every day on rapid recognition of words is almost an essential to success. For this purpose "sight cards" provide a convenient method of securing the repetition with variety which insures attention.

It must be borne in mind that phonics for reading purposes cannot be used in exactly the same way as we use it with children.

A child will recognize the phonogram "ail" and build the words "pail," "tail," by prefixing "p" or "t" and there will be a flash of recognition in his mind because the words have meaning. To the foreigner, however, such a proceeding is useless. The words which he builds or the words which he analyzes phonetically, call up no ideas. To him these words are "full of sound and fury, signifying nothing." Hence, the lesson in phonics must always lag behind the vocabulary of a foreigner.

28

Nationalities differ in the way in which they mispronounce vowels, e. g., the Italians will say: eet for it, lip for leap, mit for meat, pick for peak, etc. A device for teaching the proper pronunciation of the troublesome short i and long e, is to place the words in two columns, e. g., it—eat, and ask the pupils to pronounce the word in column 1 or in column 2. The class is then called upon to decide whether the speaker called the word in column 1; if the class decides that the speaker called the word in column 2, the former is made conscious of his mispronunciation and he will then be ready to learn the distinction. Following is a list of such words given in the New York City Syllabus:

hairs	—has	pat	—part	taught	—tot	met	—mate
hairy	—Harry	had	—hard	pawned	—pond	led	—laid
Mary	—marry	pack	—park	gnawed	—nod	pen	—pain
fairy	—ferry	match	—March	dawn	—don	fell	—fail
chair	—cheer	badge	—barge	caught	—cot	west	—waist
dip	—deep	hem	—ham	thy	—thou	pour	—paw
dim	—deem	pet	—pat	high	—how	core	—caw
bid	—bead	bed	—bad	find	—found	fort	—fought
mill	—meal	pen	—pan	mice	—mouse	lord	—laud
lick	—leak	shell	—shall	signed	—sound	soar	—saw
pitch	—peach	guess	—gas			roar	—raw
more	—mow	buck	—book	sup	—soap	pull	—pool
tore	—toe	tuck	—took	rub	—robe	full	—fool
sore	—sow	luck	—look	but	—boat	could	—cooed
bore	—bow			must	—most	would	—wooed
shore	—show					wood	—wooed

WRITTEN ENGLISH

In the earliest stages of English instruction, the written work is confined to copying and dictating. Gradually, as English loses its strangeness, original composition may be attempted. Very modest is the pupil's first attempt, for it is confined to filling in words in sentences which he has at one time read in complete form. Thus, "Do you —— the stream?" "The pen is —— the table." The pupil supplies the words "see" and "on."

With the growth of a vocabulary, the pupils may attempt to answer in writing questions such as "What is your name?" "Where do you work?" "How long have you been in the country?" "What experience have you?" "Have you any references?" The pupils should be given an opportunity to fill in blanks such as those furnished by the New York Public Library, by the Immigration Bureau, or by the Post Office. Other exercises leading up to original composition are:

(a)—Answering the questions in complete sentences, such as:
1. What is done with bread, coal, knife, ink, hat, comb, money, breakfast, apple, stove, etc.
2. What thing is red, long, short, broad, narrow, thick, thin, etc.
3. Use the following words in sentences: Today, now, soon, at once, never, always, long ago, often, sometimes, once, this time, there, here, above, below, etc.
(b)—Writing short paragraphs when the topics are furnished by the teacher.
(c)—Simple reproductions of stories.
(d)—Short letters of a very practical nature—letters ordering goods, complaining of non-delivery, applying for opening gas meter, excuse for child's absence from school, receipts. For a list of topics, see the syllabus which follows.
(e)—Sending telegrams.
(f)—Writing advertisements for situations wanted.

Utility should be the standard for the selection of all exercises. Whatever the pupil will find of value in his daily life may be taught. Nothing else ought to be considered. Whatever educational values composition has will inhere in practical work far better than in imaginative descriptions and expositions.

In connection with composition, there will arise opportunities for simple lessons in grammar. The themes have been constructed with simple sentences. As soon as pupils are ready, the uses of personal and relative pronouns may be taught. For example: "I open the door." "The door leads to the classroom." Show how the two simple sentences may be combined by means of a relative pronoun. "I open the door which leads to the classroom." The uses of conjunctions—if, therefore, because, so that, etc., are taught in the same way. The correct case forms of personal pronouns are best taught by means of sentences which require the pupils to fill in blank spaces. Thus insert

> I or me
> he or him
> she or her
> He gave the book to ———.
> We told ——— the story.

Agreement of subject and predicate, the past tenses and past participles of verbs, may be illustrated in the same way. English is "a grammarless tongue." In learning any other modern language, much time must be devoted to learning inflections and variations. In English, inflections of pronouns, changes in tense, in number, in agreement, may all be learned without drilling declensions and con-

30

jugations. Whatever grammar is taught, it is now agreed should be taught in connection with its immediate use in composition.

SPELLING

As might be expected, foreigners find great difficulty with learning how to spell. We may minimize this difficulty somewhat by selecting such words only as they would use in their written work, and not forcing them to learn how to spell every word which they meet in their reading and conversation.

The words of our vocabularies do not comprise one general list of words which serve our purposes in communicating orally and by written symbols as well as in understanding others orally and by written symbols. As a matter of fact, our vocabularies consist of four more or less distinct groups of words making up our speaking, writing, understanding, reading vocabularies. "In short, there are kinds and degrees of acquaintanceship with words as with friends. Some words are known to us only as we hear them spoken by other persons. Others are recognized in our reading but are strangers to our speaking and writing vocabularies. Finally, there are a few choice words with which we are so familiar that we use them with confidence to convey our thoughts to others. Among the latter are the words we use in writing."

Since spelling ability is of value only in writing and since immigrants have a limited need for writing in English it is apparent that our pupils need be taught the spelling of a relatively small number of words and that these words must be selected from the probable writing of the pupil rather than from his reading or understanding. Interesting studies have revealed that reading and speaking vocabularies are not affected by learning the spelling of words nor does one necessarily know how to spell words in the speaking or understanding vocabulary. The only value of spelling ability as well as its final test is in the use to which spelling is put in written communication.

Spelling lists selected from the reading and speaking vocabularies of pupils are not only likely to be too large but also likely to stress words which pupils will hardly use in their writing and to neglect words which the pupils will probably use in writing. Spelling books are not reliable sources for words as they include in their lists less than twenty per cent of words used in the writing of English-speaking men as determined by the studies of Jones, Ayres and others.

At present the most reliable lists of spelling words for our pupils are to be obtained by the teacher in choosing the words that the learners use in their written discourse. This may perhaps be supplemented by such a combined list of words as are contained in Ayers' or Chancellor's 1000 words.

One is said to know how to spell a word when one can write it automatically, i. e., when the mind is intent on the thought without being concerned with the form. In psychological terms, this means that spelling must be reduced to a habit basis, it must be relegated to the margin of consciousness so that the focus may be left free for thought. The reduction of an act to the automatic stage of habit is accomplished by the four-fold process of securing a strong initiative, focalization on the process, attentive repetition at ever lengthening intervals and never suffering an exception.

Adults who are learning English have a strong enough motive so that the artificial source of initiative need not be invoked. Their attention may be focalized on the difficult element in a word by:

1. Grouping words in families, e. g., come, some; who, whose, whom; should would; contrasting dough, rough, etc.
2. Making the difficult element vivid by means of boxing, red chalk, calling special attention to the difficulty, e. g., sep-a-rate; gramm-a-r; *know*-ledge..
3. Mnemonics for certain words frequently confused, e. g., words like believe—receive; use (ce) (li) as a means of re-calling the position of i.
4. Teaching simple rules, e. g., doubling final consonants in gladden; dropping silent e in truly.
5. Teaching homonyms, first separately, so that no confusion may arise; then when they know the words, teach them in pairs so as to bring out the difference.
6. Keep words frequently misspelled on the blackboard.
7. Each pupil to keep a list of words which he misspells.

To secure the necessary repetition:

1. Use the "multiple sense appeal," i. e., pupils spell orally, they hear the word spelled, they see it and they write it.
2. Vary the method of writing—in columns, in paragraphs, in sentence forms, use in composition.
3. Build words by adding prefixes and suffixes to the roots, e. g., porter, import, export, portables, etc.
5. Have a daily 5 minute drill on words misspelled.
6. Lastly, "never suffer an exception." The pupil must not be permitted to see a word misspelled, since the wrong form is just as likely to impress itself as the right form.

TEXT-BOOKS

Both in methods of teaching and preparing text-books, the modest purpose of English instruction for immigrants is frequently neglected. It is no part of the function of such instruction to initiate pupils into the beauties of English literature, nor are teachers called upon to play the part of the virtuoso, to arouse an appreciation for poetic diction. The most that can be accomplished in the time which the foreigner spends in the schoolroom is to give him the ability to understand conversational English, to make himself understood on a variety of every day topics and to read and write what will help him escape injury and to further his material wants. Any plans which attempt a higher ideal must for the present be characterized as Utopian.

Few text-books prepared recently, especially for the teaching of English to foreigners, are guilty of attempting the "grand style," but too many are built on the models of English primers with their puerile sentences about Jack and his dog Tray. Others have sentences constructed to make use of a vocabulary or to illustrate a grammatical rule. Two readers have word for word translations, giving the impression that every English word has its correlative in a foreign language. Some readers are devoted entirely to the teaching of civics, as if the foreigners' interest was exclusively in our legislative, judicial and executive departments. One reader very much used consists of a large number of simple sentences arranged in verse form, but without either rhyme or reason. Text-books recently published contain a large number of themes on topics of every day interest; give forms of letters, short stories, directions to be carried out, conversation to be carried on by one pupil with the rest of his class, questions to be answered by the pupil, suggestions for the use of words.

Prof. Jesperson holds that text-books should at least
1. Be connected with sensible reading.
2. Be interesting, lively, varied.
3. Contain the most necessary material of the language first, especially the material of every day language.
4. Be correct English.
5. Pass gradually from that which is easy to what is more difficult.
6. Be not without too much consideration for what is merely grammatically easy or difficult.

Most text-books have something which the intelligent teacher can use, and probably no text-book will be quite satisfactory. Teachers are today supplementing school texts by using the newspapers, pamphlets, circulars and mimeographed copies of reading lessons suitable for their pupils.

In selecting the subject matter of English lessons, whether the object be to teach talking or writing, the same principle holds true—that the more nearly the content of instruction coincides with the content which the pupil finds outside of the classroom, the better adapted is it to his needs; obversely, the more remote such content is from the direct and present interests of the pupil the more academic and stultifying it becomes. The principle is timidly applied in organizing the curriculum for children because their present interests are ephemeral and further activities problematical. The principle must be applied rigidly in selecting the content for the teaching of adults because the latter has undoubted life interests and pressing present needs. Such subjects as the following taken from text-books for adults are so remote from the immediate interests of adults learning to read English that they have no proper place in a program for beginners.

The Lion and the Mouse.
The English Colonies.
Voting.
The Village Blacksmith.
Success.

Adult immigrants learning to read English are more likely to require ability to read.

A bill of fare.
One of the many signs they see.
An application blank.
A time table.
A street car advertisement.
Newspaper headings.

It need hardly be pointed out that the content of reading should not be limited to the examples given but rather that content should lean towards rather than away from the reading which adult pupils would select for themselves without the teacher's fiat.

Thus only can teachers fulfill their two-fold functions, the one growing out of the other, 1st: that of satisfying present needs, interest and desires as a basis for, 2nd: the stimulation of new interests which must be satisfied when aroused.

A Syllabus for Teaching English to Foreigners

GENERAL DIRECTIONS

1. Plan Book.—Teachers should keep a detailed record of subject matter to be taught.
2. Pupils' Note Books.—Every student should receive a note book to be kept in school. In this book the pupil writes his themes, his spelling words, his dictation, his letters.
3. Weekly Program—At the beginning of the term, each teacher should prepare a weekly program based on the time schedule. The last 15 minutes had better be devoted to oral rather rather than to written work.
4. Blackboard Work.—Pupils are encouraged to come early by finding some interesting material on the board. As soon as regular class work starts this work is closed. Not more than 15 minutes should be allowed for this extra copying. Other devices to encourage early arrival are: correcting individual errors in composition, reading, speech; returning corrected papers only during the first 15 minutes; reading a continuous story during these 15 minutes; discussion of personal questions; submitting legal and medical questions to our lawyer and to our physician.

ORGANIZATION OF CLASSES

The best work can only be done when the teacher's energy is concentrated upon a fairly homogeneous group. Grading to secure uniformity on some vital basis is attended with serious difficulties because foreigners enter at irregular times, their progress is not uniform, they become attached to a teacher and because for economic reasons, classes must be consolidated. The most obvious controlling factor in selecting pupils for the various classes is their knowledge of English and using this as a basis, four grades designated as F^1, F^2, F^3, F^4 may be formed.

F^1 for beginners who speak little or no English.

F^2 for those who have completed F^1 or can speak fair English and can write a simple letter.

F^3 for those who have completed F^2 or can carry on conversation in English and read a newspaper.

F^4 for those who have completed F^3 or can read a paragraph aloud and give the substance.

The lower grades are further subdivided on the basis of Nationality, but no attempt should be made to separate the various nationalities in F³ and F⁴. Further subdivisions are based on age and on previous education in the pupils' native language. The complete organization for F¹ provided enough pupils attend may be illustrated as follows:

1. F¹.—Russian.—Good education.
2. F¹.— " —Poor "
3. F¹.—Ruthenian.
4. F¹.—Hungarian.
5. F¹.—German and Austrian.
6. F¹.—Italian.—Poor education—old.
7. F¹.— " — " " —young.
8. F¹.—Jewish— " " —old.
9. F¹.— " — " " —young.
10. F¹.— " —Good " — "
11. F¹.— " — " " —old.
12. F¹.—Mixed races.
13. F¹.—Illiterates.
14. F¹.—Entering class—(formed after 3 weeks).

TIME SCHEDULE

Reading	15—20	15—20	20—30	20—30
Conversation	20—30	20—30	10—15	10—15
Theme or Topic development..	20—30	15	15	15
Writing (copy, dictation letter, composition)	20—30	20—30	20—30	20—30
Language work (correction of errors and grammar)	10	10	10—20	10—20
Spelling	10	10	10	10
Phonics	5—10	5	10 weekly	10 weekly
Dictionary			10 "	10 "
Synonyms—Homonyms			10 "	10 "
Formal Civics		20 weekly	20-30 "	20-30 "
Two minute setting up exercise	2	2	2	2

The figures indicate the minimum and maximum number of minutes per night except where the number of minutes weekly is given.

No special time allotment is made for arithmetic because the subject is to be given during the oral and written English periods.

PLAN FOR INEXPERIENCED TEACHERS

Teachers without previous experience with foreign pupils are advised to use the plan which follows. By following carefully the directions and by reading the syllabus especially for F¹, the teacher will then have sufficient confidence to formulate his own plan for each evening's work. Beginning teachers are advised to consult the principal and the other teachers of their grade for suggestions.

1st evening:

   I. Greet pupils as they come in.

Tell them your name when class is assembled and write your name on the board.

From the list furnished, call the roll, e.g., "John Brown"—"stand"—Show what you mean by rising; use words of approval when they understand, e.g., "Good;" "You understand;" "Fine."

If you have no list, say to a pupil " What is your name?"
Have each pupil say "My name is————."
Check your roll as the names are given.

  II. Develop the first sentences in the theme "to open the door" or in any other theme in the suggested list. See directions for development in the course for F^1.

  III. Let pupils write their names on the papers and copy sentences from the board.

While they are working, walk around the room and learn to know your pupils. Help those who need your help.

2nd evening:

   I. Greetings. Engage pupils in conversation if possible about their affairs, e.g., their occupations, addresses, place of birth, length of time in the country.

  II. Teach "I live at————Street."
Check the addresses given, or write them on your cards. Have pupils write their addresses on paper.

  III. Review the first 5 sentences of the theme.
Complete the theme.

  IV. Introduce the 2 minute physical training drill.
Let pupils open the windows.
Say "class stand." Demonstrate the meaning of each command.
"Face the windows."
"Breathe in"—"out"—8 times.
"Face front."
"Arms upward stretch," "Down"—4 times.
"Bend trunk to the right—left"—4 times. "Class sit."

3rd evening:

   I. Greetings.

  II. Teach pupils to give their occupations. Have them write "I am a————(tailor)."

  III. Review the theme by having pupils read and act out each sentence.

  IV. Two minute drill—introduce head turning.

   V. Drill on recognition of words—select from 5 to 10 words in the theme.

VI. Teach them how to spell from 5 to 10 words in the theme.

VII. Dictate 3 sentences. Let pupils correct by comparing with copy on board.

4th evening:

I. Greetings—vary them, e.g., How do you do—Good evening: I am glad to see you.

II. Review recognition and spelling of words tonight.

III. Let pupil perform the acts described in the theme and give the sentences from memory. Help them when they forget by asking "and then?"

IV. Two minute drill—introduce knee bending.

V. Teach five to ten new words.

VI. Let pupils write as many sentences as they remember.
Let them correct by comparing with the copy on the board.

5th evening:

Proceed as before.
New material: Develop the second theme.
Spelling—ten words.
Word recognition—ten words.
Writing—I was born in——— (Sweden).
Two minute drill—introduce facing; hands on hips, on shoulders.
Conversation—Place of work, hours of employment.
Counting; concrete objects e.g. I have two hands; ten fingers; three children.

6th evening:

A proverb "Make haste slowly." Dictation of four or five sentences from theme.
Spelling—Review words taught. Select words misspelled by pupils in their dictation and memory work for future drill.
Conversations: Review subject matter so far taught.
Writing: Place on the board a summary of the conversation exercises. Leave blank spaces to be filled in by pupils. Have each pupil copy from the board and fill in the blank space e.g.

My name is..........
I live at..........
I was born in..........
I am.......... years old.
My occupation is..........

THE THEME

In the teaching of English to foreigners, the theme means a series of short related sentences on a single topic. The words "and then" are understood after each sentence so as to establish the relationship of time sequence between the ideas called forth. Furthermore, each sentence must be capable of being dramatized or illustrated graphically or mimetically. These two characteristics of the theme—sequence and possibility of dramatizing are illustrated in the following:

GETTING UP

I open my eyes at six o'clock.
I push back the covers.
I jump out of bed.
I stretch my arms.
I wash myself.
I dry myself with a towel.
I dress myself.
I eat my breakfast.

The arrangement of sentences in "theme" fashion is necessary for beginners. One sentence helps the pupil to think of the next sentence and the meaning of each sentence may be taught by other means than by translation. The theme therefore bridges the gap between the pupil and the teacher because they cannot communicate in English. But there is nothing magical in arranging sentences as in a theme nor does beginning each sentence with "I" lessen the difficulty of teaching a foreigner English. The theme as a matter of fact is useless with pupils who speak a little English and this means should not be employed beyond the first four or five weeks and then only with beginning pupils. For advanced classes, topics may be developed in the usual paragraph form or in conversational form, but the very artificial form of the theme is not used except as indicated.

The following are the steps in the complete development of the theme:

1°. The teacher performs an act, at the same time saying the words which describe the act, e.g., I open the door.
2°. Pupils perform the act and say the words.
3°. The teacher says the words and writes them on the board.
4°. Pupils read the words and perform the act.
5°. Pupils copy the theme.
6° Pupils review by going through complete dramatization description and reading. .
7°. Pupils write selected sentences from dictation and from memory.

From 5 to 10 sentences are developed in one evening.
Complete development of a theme usually takes three or four evenings.

SUGGESTED LIST OF THEMES

1. I open the door.
2. I light the gas.
3. I get up in the morning.

4. I get up.
5. I eat breakfast.
6. I go to work.
7. I begin my day's work.
8. I leave my shop and go to evening school.
9. I look for work.
10. I build a fire in my stove.
11. I receive my pay.
12. I deposit money in the bank.
13. I rent rooms.
14. I hang a picture on the wall.
15. I pay my rent (board).
16. I write and mail a letter.
17. I send money to my parents.
18. I buy shoes.
19. I go to the doctor.
20. I go to a restaurant.
21. I take the train.
22. I telephone to my friend.

VARIATION OF THEME

For review purposes the following variations are suggested:

1°. Pupil performs actions—another pupil describes them.
2°. Pupil recites the sentence, another pupil performs the actions.
3° Change the person, e.g., I go to the door. He goes to the door.
4°. Change the tense, e.g. I go to the door. I went to the door.

INCIDENTAL READING

This would include all forms of material available for a first year class outside of text-books:

1. Newspapers (see special topic).
2. Familiar signs.

The foreigner constantly sees certain signs about him with which he should be made familiar. He should be encouraged to make copies of signs he sees daily and to bring them to school. It will be surprising to one who has not tried this device to see what material will be brought to class, how beneficial this will prove and how interested the pupils will be in this kind of work.

SUGGESTED SIGNS

EXIT   ENTRANCE   THIS WAY OUT   DANGER

KEEP TO THE   LOOK OUT   LINE FORMS ON
RIGHT   FOR PAINT   THIS SIDE

PULL   TICKET OFFICE   BOX OFFICE   PUSH

NOT RESPONSIBLE FOR GOODS LEFT OVER 30 DAYS	DO NOT CROSS THE TRACKS	NO SMOKING OR CARRYING OF LIGHTED CIGARS

	PASSENGERS ARE FORBIDDEN	
KEEP OUT	TO STAND ON PLATFORMS OF TRAINS	HANDS OFF

NOT RESPONSIBLE FOR HATS AND COATS	OFFICE HOURS 9—12 A.M. 1—3 P.M.

STREET CLOSED   PRIVATE   SMOKING ROOM

COUNT YOUR CHANGE	ROOMS (APARTMENT, LOFT, ETC.) TO LET	WAITING ROOM

Some teachers may be able to secure discarded car advertisement signs. Some are very simple to read and are "Live," interesting material.

TWO MINUTE DRILL.

After the first hour have the two minute drill in every classroom. In the foreign classes this activity should well serve a twofold purpose—first, to afford relaxation and change of air and secondly, to teach the pupils the sentence structure and words in their natural setting rather than as isolated words.

Instead of having pupils learn—"This is my head; these are my arms," etc., have them learn the names of the various parts of the body by going through various exercises at the order of the teachers.

Some such orders follow—Messrs. Cohen, Smith and Brown, please open the windows.

Class, stand.

Quietly put up your seats and desks.

Turn to the right, left, to the back of the room, to the front of the room, etc.

Turn to the windows.

Breathe in through your nostrils. Breathe out through your mouth. Slowly.

Do this again.

Once more.

Turn to the front.

Heads high.

Heels together. Toes out.

Chests high.

Hands on hips place, on shoulders, on head, on ears.

This two minutes drill should be given every evening; the teacher varies the exercises to prevent automatic response without grasping the meaning of the orders and to include a vocabulary and a sentence structure applicable to most parts of the body. Examples of other exercises are:

Knee bending.
Stretch arms forward; upward.
Rise on toes.
Turn palms of hands upward.
Eyes front.

CONVERSATION

Conversation between teachers and pupils is the most natural way of teaching English and is the most valuable exercise for practical reasons. The earliest exercises are designed to furnish the teacher with necessary information about the pupils, their lives, their needs and their interests. Thus the teacher asks such questions as the following:

With whom do you board?
Where were you born?
Who is your employer?
How many hours a day do you work?
How many children have you?

A later development in the process of securing free conversation is that of questioning on the subject matter of the theme and of reading matter. Thus the pupils know the theme "Going to school."

"I put on my hat and coat. I say Good-bye.
I walk to school. I enter the building.
I come into the room."

The teacher now asks the following questions:

Mr.——do you walk to school?
Does Mr.—— walk to school?
Walk around the room, Mr——
Walk to the front of the room, Mr.——
Please put your hat on, etc.

Dramatization by 2 pupils of situations requiring conversations:

Buying a suit.
Asking one's way.
Renting a room.
Ordering a meal.
Checking a trunk.
Applying for a position.

During these dramatizations, the teacher notes errors made by the pupils. Several correct forms suggested by the class are placed on the board. Other pupils then go through the conversation using one of several correct forms. The teacher avoids monotony by first making the conversations short; second, by calling on many pupils to participate; third, by changing the subject frequently.)

In the upper grades conversation exercises are based on current events, on problems that confront the pupils, on elementary history and geography and civics. After the class has been organized and the class officers elected, the pupils are taught elementary parliamentary procedure. Later in the term, set debates are prepared by several pupils and the best debaters are selected for the inter class debates conducted toward the end of the term.

READING

Most adult foreigners, like most American children, take pleasure in reading aloud in the classroom. It is questionable whether the rest of the class derives either profit or pleasure from an exercise which usually is nothing more than a series of mispronunciations. No one "gets thought from the printed page" by this process. Progressive teachers have gradually abandoned the attempt to get meanings by calling words and as a result are insisting on silent rather than oral reading because their pupils outside school will read silently and not orally.

The following will suggest means to getting the thought:

1. Introducing the reading lesson by the teacher.
2. Reading aloud by the teacher.
3. Explanation of difficult words and expressions.
4. Pupils read silently.
5. Reproduction of subject matter read.
6. Questions on the context.

Pupils read aloud:

1. When all books except that of the reader are closed.
2. When a pupil has prepared a selection for oral reading from newspaper, magazine or other text-book.
3. When the rest of the class is busy at something else, a poor reader may be called upon to read aloud to the teacher.

The first reading material is the subject matter developed on the board. Books are used after two or three weeks but the pupils are encouraged to read silently and to talk about the reading matter rather than to read aloud. Reading from pamphlets, circulars, signs, blackboard is of even greater value than reading from a text-book.

READING A NEWSPAPER

With the average first year foreign class little or no use can be made of the English newspaper. However, towards the close of the school year when most of the "visitors" have dropped out and the cream of the pupils are left, the newspaper may be brought in to teach pupils how to find useful information such as:

1. Arrival and departure of ships.
2. Weather conditions.
3. Help wanted ads.
4. Business troubles.

A glance through any daily paper will enable the teacher to collect just what items would be of interest to his particular class.

PHONICS

For the teacher of English to Foreigners, phonic drill serves two distinct purposes, viz.,

1. To correct foreign accent, enunciation and pronunciation.
2. To furnish a key for the recognition of new words.

Judged by the results obtained, it is questionable whether correcting foreign pronunciation in adult pupils deserves the time usually devoted to it. Habits are too firmly fixed to be eradicated in the short time spent by foreigners in our Evening Schools. The time required for this purpose may usually be more profitably spent in teaching pupils to communicate their ideas even though perfection be not attained. Some corrective exercises, however, are desirable to prevent ambiguity and to correct certain racial characteristics which may easily be corrected. Such errors needing attention are:

1. Upward inflection in statements.
2. Sing song.
3. Guttural sounds of R.
4. Confusion of certain sounds:

> Long *e* and *i—eet* for *it*.
> Short *o* and *i—som* for *some*.
> *t* and *th—tank* for *thank*.
> *w* and *wh—wen* for *when*.
> *v* and *w—vay* for *way*.
> *f* and *v—fine* for *vine*.
> *gs* and *gz—eksact* for *egzact*.
> *j* and *ch—chust* for *just*.
> *s* and *z—iss* for *iz*.
> *oi* and *or—woik* for *work*.
> *e* and *a—men* for *man*.
> *ing* for *ink—kink* for *king*.
> *th* and *f—fru* for *thru*.

To correct such errors, the teacher should know the position of the mouth parts in forming the sounds. A good chart for this purpose will be found on pages 16-17. Very many helpful devices will be found in Maxwell, Barnum and Johnson.—Speaking and Writing, and in Hervey Hix.—Lesson Plans for Teachers.

Furnishing a key for the pronunciation of new words is the second purpose of phonic drill. The procedure is as follows:

1. Pupils learn to recognize and to pronounce about 100 words in their themes. These words are recognized as wholes without any phonic analysis just as faces are recognized as wholes without analysis of the various facial parts.

2. Troublesome words are grouped in families, e.g., who, whose, whom, hands, lands, bands.

3. Picking out phonic elements, e.g., the sound of an, ing, squ.

4. Forming new words by combining with other sounds, e.g., and with t, c, f, beg.

5. Modifying the sound by the addition of silent e, e.g., can—cane; bit—bite; cut—cute.

Caution: The new words formed must be in the vocabulary of the learner.

The following list of phonic elements will serve as a guide. The order of teaching will depend entirely in the words which the pupils know.

An, at, ad, ab, ack, am, amp. The same final consonants with e, i, o, u, ess, oud, an, urn, ook, ash, ink, ing, ew, ould, ance, aco, atch, squ, ough, eigh, ove, ow.

CIVICS

Civics should be taught in every grade. Included in the term "Civics" is everything that will make the foreigner a better member of the community, a better worker, a better husband and father, as well as a more intelligent voter. The latter aspect of civics are reserved for grades F^2, F^3 and F^4 because the pupil must have a fair command of English to understand the constitution and the provisions for government.

Memory Gems

Proverbs and short sayings are memorized after they have been developed and their meanings made clear by anecdote or illustration. Pupils are encouraged to use them in talking and to give illustrations from their own experience. A suggested list of proverbs follows:

Haste makes waste.
The only way to have a friend is to be one.
A good name is better than great riches.
Never spend your money before you have it.
Speech is silver, silence is gold.
Look before you leap.
A stitch in time saves nine.
Do not cry over spilt milk.
Birds of a feather flock together.
Never find pleasure in another's misfortune.

45

Rome was not built in one day.

One today is worth two tomorrows.

Health is better than wealth.

Do to others as you would have others do to you.

It is never too late to learn.

Better late than never.

A penny saved is a penny earned.

Save the pennies and the dollars will take care of themselves.

Enough is better than too much.

Do as you would have others do to you.

An empty barrel makes the loudest noise.

Look up and not down.

Look forward and not backward.

Always lend a helping hand.

Do not count your chickens before they are hatched.

A place for everything and everything in its place.

Never put off till tomorrow what you can do today.

Deeds are greater than words.

Well begun is half done.

When the cat's away, the mice will play.

You cannot eat your cake and have it too.

Many hands make light work.

Kind words never die.

Honor thy father and thy mother.

Every little helps.

Think twice before you speak once.

It is never too late to mend.

The early bird catches the worm.

A soft answer turneth away wrath.

All things come to him who waits.

Lost time is never found again.

All that glitters is not gold.

He who cannot obey cannot command.

God helps those who help themselves.

Better alone than in bad company.

Live for something, do not be idle.

The United States is a government of the people, by the people, and for the people.

Correction of Errors

No list of ready made errors to be corrected can be of great value to the teacher except in pointing out types of errors to be guarded against. The following list of typical foreignisms is intended as notice to the teacher to be on guard against such expressions and to give definite instruction in eradicating these errors when they are found in his classroom. The teacher will of course correct any other foreign or unidiomatic expressions as they occur.

FOREIGN EXPRESSIONS FOR CORRECTION

Prepositions

I was by my daughter.
He took it off me.
He stole it on me.
What's the matter of you.
I ought to of gone.
It was surrounded of mountains.
He came near to him.
I am not afraid of to work.
For reference, I can get off my Teacher.
I am not sorry off it.

She was interested to the exciting story.
Subtract 7 by 12.
We bought it by a butcher.
He went on a party.
Don't be angry on me.
Why you laught from me.
He looks different than me.
They took it off'n him.
This dress is from silk.
They enjoyed very much on a ball.

Tense

If he would have done....
I am here since 2 years.
He come home late.
He is strong like.

I had a right to go (I should have gone).
If it will continue (if it continue).
He works like he doesn't like it.

Miscellaneous

Yesterday night.
My pencil is failing.
He paid for the eats.
I put myself on.
You have too much pencils.
My brother is getting 6 years old.
It stands so in the book.
He always begins with me (annoys).
He extra did it.
They made from me a captain.
We stood up late.
I got yet more money.
She goes nice dressed.
He bought for 5 cents candy.
The policeman took him arrested.
The milk is kind of sour.
A book fails me.
Leave me go.
Borrow me a nickel.
I talk so good like you.

Yours respectively.
I am interesting in the story.
The compass what I took.
I stood in the class (remain).
To my opinion.
A women.
The ship became out of motion.
Spill the mixture in the sink.
They were all talking to once.
I am finished.
Give him eats.
Mexico fighting between her own self.
His stockings were with big holes through.
Not every house there is in here bells.
He was sick on the throat.
It stands written in the book.

SPELLING

Pupils learn how to spell those words which they use or expect to use in writing. Words are not properly on the spelling list merely because they occur in reading or in any other subject matter. The basis of selection is usefulness in writing. Since it is fair to assume that foreigners learning English will have a very limited need for writing in English, each teacher selects for spelling words from the actual written work of the pupils.

As a result of a study of letters written by foreigners, the following list of misspelled words is submitted for review purposes:

Words misspelled by Foreigners

assessment	deserve	need	satisfy
attend	discharge	obliged	Sunday
advise	dropping	ordered	supply
address	employed	paid	some
attention	evening	possible	them
anxious	experience	please	think
away	friend	place	tell
and	forgive	obliging	too
able	from	position	trouble
against	find	package	this
attract	following	respectfully	their
advance	give	receipt	time
accept	gentlemen	remind	that's
arrived	getting	read	truly
afternoon	greatly	reason	take
brotherhood	hope	received	thousand
back	heard	request	thanking
big	haven't	receive	told
because	hear	remain	Tuesday
become	it	recommendation	tailor
business	imagine	ready	unsatisfied
black	interesting	striking	vacation
crown	in (for and)	send	very
card	is (his)	sent	whole
clerk	immediate	suffer	which
corner	if (ef)	see	when
can't	live	success	working
couldn't	lands	said	write
come	learn	season	what
collection	last	society	was
change	language	stock	why
cloth	life	suits	will
citizen	months	sorry	Wednesday
circumstances	man	system	worry
cause	meeting	struggle	with
certify	made	settle	want
don't	necessary	sir	well
decide	nay	study	your

A pupil knows how to spell when he can write words in context. Teaching a pupil how to spell involves two processes. 1st Focalization, or pointing out. 2nd Drill, reducing the spelling of words to habitual or automatic reactions.

For the first step, the following devices are usually employed.

1st Underscoring the confusing letter or syllable.
2nd Contrasts, e.g., there—their.
3rd Marking the difficulty in color.
4th Keeping the words before pupils.
5th Using mnemonics, e.g., for *pieces;* ei and ie after l and c.
6th Teaching simple rules, e.g. The rule for doubling final consonants when a syllable is added.

The second step involves sufficient drill so that a pupil acquires the habit of writing words correctly in sentences. Means to this end are:

1st Oral spelling; 2nd Writing words in columns, in paragraphs; 3rd Dictation exercised using words to be spelled; 4th Forming derivatives; 5th Arranging words in families.

COMPOSITION

Writing in English serves both as a means and as an end. As a means, pupils write to drill the words and sentences of use to them in oral discourse. As an end, pupils write to convey their thoughts in English. All foreign pupils require writing for drill on language forms, but they have a very limited need for communicating their thoughts in written English. A study conducted for the purpose of determining what kind of writing is needed and demanded by foreign pupils, disclosed the startling fact that no one asked for compositions on topics such as are usually assigned but that all wanted to be taught letter writing. Furthermore, less than 10% of the pupils wished to write personal letters because they preferred to use their native tongue in writing to relatives and friends; the rest wished to be taught simple business letters which could not be written in a foreign language.

The suggestions which follow seek to meet the needs of the pupils. The order of difficulty in teaching pupils to communicate their thoughts is followed:

1. Copying from the board into note books; not more than 5 sentences during one lesson.

2. Filling blank spaces to use words taught.
   i.e. I sit.... a table.
   I wipe my face with a....
   A.... is used for cutting.

3. Answering questions in writing, e.g.
   What is your name?
   Where do you live?
   How old are you?

Where do you work?

Who is your employer?

4. Filling in application blanks for postal money orders, library cards, declaration of intention, application for license, application for workmen's compensation.

5. Dictation of easy sentences, corrected from model on the board.

6. Reproduction of themes from memory.

7. Writing short business letters after a model has been presented on the board. To prevent confusion in the minds of the pupils the following form is uniformly taught:

155 E. 4th Street,

New York City,

April 24, 1917.

Mr. John Brown,

450 Broadway,

New York City.

Dear Sir:—

....

....

....

Yours truly,

Henry Smith.

From the following list the teacher selects such forms as will be of use to his pupils. The list is suggestive only and does not prevent the teaching of other useful letters.

LETTER FORMS

Letters of application—

For a position (only such trades as apply in writing).

Increase in salary.

License to——— (peddle, sell perishable foods).

Membership in———(society, club, lodge).

A letter of recommendation.

Letter of Excuse for—

Absence from school.

A child's absence from school.

Failure to go to work.

Failure to do a required work.

Letters of inquiry about—

The cost of goods, board, lodging, insurance (fire, life).
Desirable forms of insurance policies.
Rights under various clauses of insurance policies.
Amount due insured on his policy.
Interpretation of—Workingmen's Compensation Law.
The work of———— in school.

Letters of requests for—

Business or school catalogue, fashion book, circular or railroad guide.
Samples.
Price list discounts.
Declaration of intention.
Rates for installing—(machinery, fire sprinkler, etc.).
Copies of free publications.
Repair man, e.g., Gas Co., landlord.

Letters reporting—

Loss of parcel in street car.
Sickness—to employer, to lodge.
Accident—to Compensation Commission.
Fire—to Insurance Co.

Letters of complaint—

To a Municipal Department—garbage not removed, dark halls, obstructed stairways, failure to report contagious diseases.
To Public Service Com.—Overcharge by Gas Co. Insufficient heat in cars.
To Post Office or Express Co., money order lost, not paid.
To a mercantile house—overcharge; goods not delivered; quality not satisfactory; package broken; lack of courteous treatment.

Notices—

Of removal.
Formation of firm.
Change of business detail (price, discount, kind of goods, etc.),
New styles.
Lodge meeting.

Sales Letters—

Simple letter offering goods for sale.

Ordering Goods—

By description; by reference to catalogues, by reference to previous transactions; duplication of orders.

Acknowledgments—

Receipt of check, money or money order; receipt of goods.

Dunning Letters—

Request for salary overdue; for money loaned; for money due in business transactions. Follow up letters.

Formal notes—

Of invitation, e.g., wedding; confirmation, acceptance, declination; announcements; e.g., wedding, birth.

ARITHMETIC

Under this heading, the following work is done with first year foreign students.

1. Reading and writing of numbers—ordinal and cardinal, taught by the conversational method only. How many fingers have you? How many cents in a dime? How old are you?
2. Telling time.
3. Meaning of signs such as $, c., 2 for 3c.; 10c. doz.; $1.98.
4. Writing and reading such signs.
5. Making and understanding checks, bills, and receipts, postal money orders.

THEMES FOR FIRST YEAR CLASSES
Light the Fire

I get out of bed.
The house is very cold. My room is cold.
I take some newspaper.
I put the paper into the stove.
I place some dry wood on top of the paper.
I strike a match and light the fire.
The fire burns briskly, (brightly).
Then I put some coal on the fire.
The fire warms the room.

I Get Up In the Morning

I look at my watch.
I jump out of bed.
I put on my clothes.
I wash my face, hands and neck.
I put on my collar and tie.
I clean my teeth.
Then I brush and comb my hair.
Now I go to the dining room for breakfast.

I Go to Work

I leave my house at seven o'clock to go to work.
I work at Third Avenue and 59th Street.
I walk to Second Avenue, corner of Fifth Street.
I see a car coming.
I go into the street from the sidewalk.

I signal the motorman.
He stops his car.
I enter the car and pay my fare.
I ride to 59th Street.
I leave the car.

I Wash My Hands

I go to the sink.
I roll up my sleeves.
I turn on the water.
I take a piece of soap.
I hold the soap under the running water.
I rub the soap with my hands.
I wash my hands in the water.
I turn off the water.
I dry my hands with the towel.
I roll down my sleeves.

PARAGRAPHS DEVELOPED IN CONVERSATION
To Buy Shoes

I have a pair of torn shoes.
The streets are wet from a heavy rain.
I do not want to have wet feet.
I go to a shoe store in my neighborhood.
"What do you want?"
"I want a pair of shoes."
"What kind do you want?"
"I want a pair of lace shoes."
He takes my size and tries on a pair of lace shoes.
I am satisfied with these shoes.
I give him the money and walk out of the store.
I have new shoes.

Noon-Hour.

The factory whistle blows. It is twelve o'clock.
I feel hungry. I have worked hard all morning.
I take off my working clothes, go to the sink, wash my hands and face.
I feel fresher now.
I go to the nearest restaurant. The food is clean. The service is clean.
I order my lunch.
I eat slowly.
I finish my meal and take a slow walk back to the shop.

SECOND YEAR (F²)

Pupils in this grade have either completed F¹ or can speak and read English fairly well.

Oral Composition:

Useful subject matter is developed by questions from the teacher and the answers written in paragraph form on the board. The class reads, asks questions and finally copies the work on the board into their note books. Suggestions for the topics used for development are:

Hygiene—How to ventilate a room; keeping food clean.

Economy—High cost of living. Planning expenditures; Municipal market; food dictators, where to put savings.

Industry—Preparation for better position; industrial centers; wages in different trades; health consideration in occupations.

Aesthetics—Museums; places of amusement; places to visit; public concerts.

Education—Pre-vocational, vocational, technical and agricultural schools; scholarships in schools and in colleges.

History—Brief biographies of national heroes in connection with national celebrations.

Civics—The Post Office; the Library; City hospitals, dispensaries; the Police Department; Tenement House department; Municipal ordinances, e.g., spitting, carrying fire arms, obstructing fire escapes; congregating; selling spoilt food; licenses.

Conversation:

Special emphasis on dramatization of actual situations requiring English conversation. Two or more pupils conduct a brief conversation, the teacher notes errors and suggests variant methods for expressing the ideas.

Suggested topics:

Exchanging an article in a department store.
Buying an article.
Asking one's way.
Requesting an increase in salary; a day off.
Offering an excuse or apology.
Greeting.

Spelling:

See list of words frequently misspelled.
Words selected from the written work of the pupils.
Difficulties pointed out; words drilled orally and in written sentences.

Phonics:

Correction of errors in pupils' conversation and in oral reading. Review of difficult phonograms, see F¹.

Language forms and Grammar:

1. Only so much grammar is taught as will be immediately applied by foreigners in written and in spoken English, e.g. Plural of

nouns are taught in sentences so as to associate the correct forms of nouns and verbs.

2. The past and future tenses in sentences containing adverbs of time, e.g., He went to the shop yesterday, last week, a year ago. I shall go to work tomorrow, when I feel well; later.

3. The genders of simple nouns, e.g. man—woman; cock—hen; boy—girl; bachelor—man; father—mother; bull—cow; king—queen; master—mistress; son—daughter; uncle—aunt; widower—widow; Jew—Jewess; heir—heiress; lion—lioness; actor—actress; prince—princess.

4. The use of personal pronouns to represent an antecedent, e.g. This man wants a job. *He* is a good workman. *He* has a little sister. Do you know *her? His* father and *his* mother came to America. *They* are good people. *Your* coat is torn. *It* needs mending.

5. The use of possessive nouns and pronouns.

6. Simple and progressive forms of verbs contrasted and explained in sentences, e. g.,

> He works every day.
> He is working now, at this time.

7. The use of *do* and *have* in questions.

8. The force of the conjunctions, and, or, but, not only, but also; either, or, neither, nor; both, and, and such subordinate conjunctions as the pupils require in expressing their thought.

9. Comparison of adjectives and adverbs in sentences.

Written Work:

1. Copying paragraph developed on the blackboard.

2. Filling blank spaces, e.g.

> The.......... bakes bread.
> We buy meat from the........
> A knife is used for........
> I wear a.......... on my head.

3. Dictation of short paragraphs or sentences having for their object (1) drill on words frequently misspelled, (2) capitalization, (3) punctuation.

4. Writing of short business letters after models have been presented. See list of suggested topics.

5. Writing original compositions on topics developed orally. Two or three compositions are written on the board and are corrected by the teacher in the presence of the class. The other compositions are corrected by the teacher and returned to the pupils. From these compositions and from the letter the teacher selects words for spelling drill and sentence structures for correction.

6. Abbreviations: The names of states and of such common words as the pupils are likely to need, e.g.

Mr.	Supt.	B. C.
Mrs.	M. D.	amt.
Gov.	Oz.	etc.
P. O.	A. D.	

7. Usual Contractions, e.g.
   I've, He doesn't, They can't, I'll go, He's, You're, I'm, it's.

8. Punctuation: The use of quotation marks, question marks, periods and commas.

9. Capitalization; The first word in a sentence, I, proper nouns and adjectives, North, East, South, West.

Reading:

For general directions see F[1].

Subject matter and vocabulary are somewhat more difficult.

The teacher judges the reading material by the following

Standards: 1st—Its interest to the class of pupils taught.

2nd—Its value to the pupils.

Excellent selections are obtained in historical and geographical readers in pamphlets and circulars freely distributed (see pamphlets of the Sons of the American Revolution). Toward the end of the term, the reading of a newspaper once a week is attempted.

Memorizing

Short saying and mottoes. Biblical proverbs. Extracts from famous speeches. Brief verses within the comprehension of the pupils.

Arithmetic:

Easy problems involving fundamental processes. The emphasis is on understanding the problems and the transactions involved rather than on securing accuracy and speed in solving. The commonly used tables, e.g.

$$12 \text{ in.} = 1 \text{ foot}$$
$$36 \text{ in.} = 1 \text{ yard}$$
$$\text{A city lot} = 25 \text{ ft. x } 100 \text{ ft.}$$
$$2 \text{ pints} = 1 \text{ quart}$$
$$4 \text{ quarts} = 1 \text{ gallon}$$
$$8 \text{ quarts} = 1 \text{ peck}$$
$$4 \text{ pecks} = 1 \text{ bushel}$$

TOPICS DEVELOPED IN CONVERSATIONS

Looking for Work

The best thing for a man to do who is out of work and looking for a good position is to buy a morning newspaper. Turn to the sheet which has the "Help Wanted" advertisements. Select one which you like and put the name and address on a piece of paper.

You then go to that place and ask to see the boss or manager. He will ask you many questions about your experience, wages, and references. Be sure and tell the truth because he will investigate what you tell him.

The boss then says to you that he will write you in a few days. If he is satisfied with you he will send you a postal card asking you to come to work.

Taking out a Library Card.

If you would like to take books from the library, go to the library. Tell the librarian what you want. She will give you a paper on which you write your name, address, occupation, place of business and also the name and address of your reference.

In a week, you go back to the library. If everything is all right, you will be given a card. With this card, you may take out books.

Going to a Doctor

The man feels sick. He cannot eat or sleep. He is too weak to work. He is seriously ill. His friends advise him to go to the doctor. He tells the doctor he does not feel well. The doctor examines his patient. He uses his instruments to find the cause of the illness. He tells the man why he is sick. He writes out a prescription. This is for the medicine. The man must take this medicine to be cured.

The Newspaper

The newspaper is a printed sheet of paper. It gives us an account of all the events of the day. Each newspaper has a great many reporters. It is the business of the reporters to find out what is going on. If there is a great fire in the city a reporter describes it. The next morning the paper will give an account of it.

The newspaper also tells about commerce, national and foreign affairs, music, politics, and sports. The newspapers contain a great many advertisements. Each newspaper is in charge of editors and managers. Some editors write editorials upon public affairs. The newsboys sell the papers on the street.

The High Cost of Living

Everybody is complaining that the cost of living is going up. Everything costs more than it did a year ago. Fish, meat, bread, eggs, milk, fruit, clothes, coal, rent,—all are now dearer. But wages too have been raised. The country is prosperous. Everyone is buying and selling. Almost everyone is making money and spending it.

The Strike

When our union struck yesterday, I could not make up my mind to join the strikers. They demanded higher wages, shorter hours of work, and more sanitary shops. I desired all that, too. But they wanted our employer to recognize the union. He refused, he said, because he had had experiences with other unions, and he thought they were all bad. Perhaps he will change his mind.

How to keep well and prevent Consumption.

Consumption is spread by careless spitting. Spittle on the floors of rooms, halls, stores and cars dries and then it will certainly be breathed in the form of dust. One should be very careful about this.

Plenty of fresh air and sunshine is the only cure for consumption. Fresh air and sunshine are the two most essential things to good health.

Night air is as good as air during the day. A person should breathe only through the nose. Try to avoid rooms that are hot, crowded, dusty and damp. Live on plain food and eat regularly. Chew the food well and slowly. Do not use ice-water.

The window of the room should be open, especially when you sleep. You should never sleep in your clothing. Be sure the clothing is dry. Damp clothing and wet feet are very injurious.

Care of the Teeth

We should pay a great deal of attention to our teeth. The teeth are covered with a hard substance called enamel.

Some of the food that we eat always sticks to our teeth. If we do not remove the food it decays, and the germs begin to eat away the enamel of our teeth. Once the enamel is eaten off by the germs, the teeth easily decay.

We must therefore remove all particles of food from our teeth.

The best way to do it is to brush our teeth before going to bed and when getting up in the morning.

Exercise

Exercise is necessary to good health. By exercising properly we strengthen our muscles, expand our lungs and chest, and improve the condition of the heart.

Deep breathing helps to purify our blood.

Walking, running, jumping, and other exercises increase the circulation of the blood.

It is therefore very important to do daily exercise..

Walking is considered to be the best exercise.

THIRD YEAR (F³)

Subjects for Oral Composition:

Current topics—educational, economic, industrial, political, historical, geographic; Safety First requirements, Fire Prevention; the work of Municipal depts; workmen's compensation.

Topics are developed and then written on the board; pupils discuss, read and copy. The sentence structure should be illustrations of the grammatical principles taught, e.g., The use of capitals; quotation marks; complex sentences showing variety in the use of conjunctions; the infinitive for the noun participle to secure variety; the proper use of shall, will; in, into, between, among.

Conversation:

1. Class discussion on topics suggested and on topics of personal interest.

2. Short stories prepared by the pupils and told in class.

3. Short debates on current topics.

Spelling: words selected from the written work of the grade. See list of words misspelled by foreigners.

Written Composition:

Emphasis on letter writing of a very practical nature. See list of suggested topics.

Development of written outlines after oral discussion of new subject matter.

Compositions on useful subjects from outlines developed on the board.

Variety in compositions may be secured by suggesting different ways of beginning, of ending; by changing structure, by expanding a short statement, by condensing a long one.

Dictation:

Short selections for the purpose of illustrating a rule or principle in grammar, punctuation; for teaching the use of words; for testing spelling.

Reading:

See F[1] for suggestions as to method.

Newspaper and magazine articles are read at least once a week. Articles are read for their interest and because they furnish desirable information; advertisements offering positions; offering land for sale; business opportunities; important news items; simple editorials.

Text-books like the Gulick Hygiene Series, Wallach's Citizenship and Strantenmuller's Home Geography give excellent material for reading.

Memorizing;

Short sayings and mottoes, Biblical proverbs, short poetical and prose selections.

Prefixes and Suffixes:

un	dis	er—or
im	out	ish
re	a	ize
over	sub	ard
ante	ex	less
pre	ing	dom
under	ist	en
ad	ness	

Homonyms:

Only such words as are frequently used:

piece—peace	cent—sent
see—sea	right—write
meat—meet	principle—principal
seen—scene	air—heir

Arithmetic:

Problems involving fractions; one or more processes. It is more important that the pupil understand the nature of the transaction involved than that he obtain a correct answer. Hence most of the arithmetic takes the form of language lessons on the problem with incidental solutions of the problems. No time is wasted on long problems or on problems involving arithmetical difficulty. The figures given are such as are usually found in the transactions involved.

TOPICS FOR READING DISCUSSION AND DRAMATIZATION

Sending Money to the Old Country

"Good evening, Mr. Smith, how do you do?"

"Very well, thank you. How are you?"

"Thanks. I am quite well. Can you tell me how to send money to my parents in the old country?"

"Certainly. I shall be glad to explain. Go to the Post Office and find the money order window. You may have to stand in line for some time."

"What shall I do when it is my turn?"

'Give your money to the clerk and tell him the name and address of your parents to whom you send the money."

"Does the clerk give me a receipt?"

"Yes. Keep it to show that you paid the money. The Post Office will then send the money safely to your parents."

"Thank you very much."

"You're quite welcome."

A Telephone Conversation

"Did you call me up this morning?"

"Yes, I asked Central to connect me with Orchard 5941, but she answered "The wire is busy." I waited a few minutes and again dropped the coin into the slot. This time the wire was not busy. I asked for you but your brother answered the 'phone."

"What did he say "

He told me to hold the wire while he looked for you. He soon came back and told me you had gone."

"I am very sorry I missed you but I had to keep an important appointment when you called me up."

A Good Salesman

"What work do you do, Jack?"

"I am a salesman in a large store."

"Do you like your work?"

"Yes, my work is quite interesting. I meet all kinds of people and I must know how to get along with them."

"What must you know in order to become a good salesman?"

"You must know the stock, the price and the quality of the goods you are selling. What is most important of all, is that you must be patient, polite and cheerful.

"Do you work in a one-price store?"

"Yes, I am very fortunate in working in a one-price store, as I do not have to haggle with my customers."

Opportunities for Advancement

This country has been called the land of opportunity. There is much truth in this statement. Hardly any other country gives its people so many opportunities to improve their condition.

Every year more and more well paid positions are offered to able and ambitious men and women. Hundreds of thousands have positions in the city, state and federal civil service. Everybody is allowed to take civil service examinations, provided he is a citizen and has the required education. The best candidates are then selected.

Evening Schools

A very important part of the work of the Board of Education is done in the Evening Schools. The most interesting of Evening Schools are those where English is taught to foreigners.

Here, men from other countries are taught to speak, read and write our language. In a few years most of them learn to do these things very well. Many pupils even go to Evening Schools later.

In this way, our Government tries to help new citizens.

What Unions Have Done

We usually think of a union as a means for getting more money for the worker. It is true that unions try to get better wages for their members but unions have done some things of greater value. They have made working conditions better. They have reduced the number of hours of labor. Furthermore, unions have improved the sanitary conditions in the shops by making the shops clean, light and airy. They have reduced the danger from fire and from accidents in handling dangerous machinery. They have installed many safety devices to prevent accidents.

Prevention of Sale of Spoiled Food.

Rotten and unclean food, sold to the innocent purchaser, causes much sickness, and sometimes, death.

What does the city do to keep bad food from being sold? The Dep't of Health employs Food Inspectors. Those men go to the different food markets, stores and pushcarts and examine the food which is being sold.

If the food looks bad or is spoiled or rotten, the inspectors take it away; and it is later thrown into the river. In some cases the people who try to sell rotten food are arrested and fined.

Prices of foods are so high, that a purchaser should get the best and cleanest for his money. Good, clean food, well cooked and chewed means good health. The city is trying to help you. Help the city by refusing to buy spoiled or rotten food, even if it is cheap.

Connected Sentences Showing the Use of Words Italicised

Last night I gave a book to *my* brother. I told *him* to read this book. *Those* volumes I liked very much.

Today, I finished reading *them*. I went back to my brother and said, "*These* books are *yours*. Will you let me have *mine?*" He answered, "Yes, I will give you *your* books. Our sister wants to read *those* books which you have in *your* hand." So, I gave *them* to him, because I wanted my sister to have them.

After this my brother and I went down to see *our* parents. You know the house *we* live in belongs to *us*. *That* house over there is *ours* also.

My sister and brother together own an auto. *Their* auto is not as good as mine. *Theirs* costs less than *ours*.

Americanism

America stands for democracy, freedom, equal chances for all. America also stands for humanity, that is, humane treatment of all persons.

Any foreigner who has a good character and believes in Government for the people and by the people, who becomes a citizen of the United States is an American. He has as much chance as anybody to advance himself and to reach any position that he is able to hold.

Any person regardless of color, race or religion, has a chance here. Notice the difference between the United States and Russia.

Employment in the United States

The U. S. is so large a country that people can find work at many trades and in many industries.

In the western part, there are many high mountains from which men dig gold, copper and other metals. We find many farms there.

In the central part, the land is flat and people raise cattle.

In the eastern part, we find coal mines, farming and manufacturing. The most important occupation is manufacturing because this part of the country 'is nearest to Europe. Much of our trade is carried on with Europe.

FOURTH YEAR (F⁴)

Conversation

Based on reading from the text, from newspapers and on current topics of interest.

The following suggestions are offered.

1°. Pupils to tell short anecdotes.—humorous—serious—personal.
2°. Summary of lessons.
3°. Dramatization of events discussed. .
4°. Original speeches.
5°. Debates—in the class; between classes.

Increasing vocabulary

1. By learning proper use of subordinate conjunctions and of transitional words.

Likewise	so then	at the same time
wherefore	too	for all that
further	only	on the contrary
moreover	then	because of which
either	yea	on the other hand
thus	similarly	in addition
so	secondly	in consequence
whence	so that	on this account
notwithstanding	yet	in spite of this
besides	again	

2. By studying the dictionary. —
3. By study of synonyms.
4. By varying expressions as found in reading matter—condensation of sentences into words or phrases; changing construction, e.g., the method of beginning; the order of words.
5. By summarizing reading matter.
6. By writing.
7. By arousing curiosity as to the meanings of words.
8. By having pupils carry a small note book for words acquired.

Formal Grammar

A review of the 8 parts of speech; sentences classified as simple, compound, and complex;

Subject, predicate, predicate noun and predicate adjective; object of verb; object of preposition.

Review of tense; the uses of shall and will..

Use of words; in sentences—

Loan	sit	liable	set
likely	learn	in	teach
into	lend	lay	borrow
lie			

Case forms in such sentences as—
This is a matter between you and—(I, me).
It is—(he, him).
He is a better man than (I, me).
(Who, whom) did you say is here?
You and—(she, her) can enter.
He is the man (who, whom) I think will be discharged.
I shall go with you and she—her.
Singular and plurals (*when used with*), each—every, no, as well as.
A man and a woman (was, were) brought in.
Every man and every woman (was, were) discharged.
Either the man or the girl (go, goes).
John as well as Frank (is, are) mistaken..
The captain with all his sailors (was, were) lost.
Every man in the school (seem, seems) happy.
A stay of several years away from home (has, have) made him
homesick.
Not one of the men (was, were) there.

Antecedents:

Let each of us do (his, their) duty.
Every plant and every animal produces after (their, its) kind.
No citizen can afford to fail in (his, their) duty.
Very few of us can do as (they, he) (wish, wishes).
Not one of the men (was, were) kept.

Prefixes and Suffixes:

en	pòst	ary
fore	pre	ous
mis	semi	some
ad	trans	ence
co-con-com	bi	ion
circum	full	ate
de	ant	ance
in-il-ig-ir	able-ible	ive
inter		

Arithmetic:

Problems involving percentage and its application in profit-loss;
insurance; interest; discount.

The direct cases alone are taught. See F³ for suggestion as to the
nature of problems.

Memorizing:

Same as F³
Selections from famous state papers.
Selections from Shakspere.

Reading.

Easy prose masterpieces such as Hale's "A man without a country;" Franklin's "Autobiography," Longfellow's "Tales of a Wayside Inn," Elbert Hubbard "A message to Garcia."

Short Poems

Hunt—About Ben Adhem.
Whitman—Captain, My Captain.
Tennyson—Sweet and Low.
Sill—Opportunity.
Longfellow—Paul Revere's Ride.

Speeches

Lincoln's Gettysburg Address.
Patrick Henry—Speech in the Virginia Convention.

State Papers

The Declaration of Independence.
Selections from the Constitution of the United States.

Newspapers and Magazines

Once a week, the class should be taught how to read a newspaper. Editorials and news items should be read and discussed in class.

Spelling

Words taken from pupils written work.
For review purposes, the list of words frequently misspelled is used.
For suggestions on drill see F¹.

Composition

Letter writing—see suggested topics.
Outlines for compositions to be delivered orally.
Summaries and reviews of lessons in other subjects.
Dictation of short paragraphs to illustrate a definite principle or rule in grammar or punctuation or for drilling the spelling of words written in content.

Homonyms

Only words commonly confused are taught:
e.g., pair—pear; bear—bare; to, too, two; eight, ate; their—there; waste—waist; hole—whole; wear—ware.

Synonyms

These are taught, (1) by illustrating each in a sentence, (2) by exact definition, (3) by use in sentence by the pupil.

Use of the Dictionary

Pupils arrange words beginning with the same letter; beginning with different letters.
Practice in finding words; in fitting meanings to context; in finding synonyms, in accenting and enunciating words.

Correct Use of Words
Choice of Prepositions

Choose the proper prepositions in the following sentences:

1. (In, into). Come——the house, and see what I have——my desk. Who has been looking——my desk Throw this paper—— the fire. There is a fire——the next room. Take this box——the bedroom and put it——the closet. Have you been playing——the street?

2. (Between, among). There has been war——France and Germany. ——you and me, I think the apples should have been divided ——the five boys equally. I saw——the crowd who stood——the tree and the house.

3. (By, with). The chair was mended——Mr. Smith——glue. The man struck me——his cane. He was displeased—— my conduct. He was punished——his father.

BIBLIOGRAPHY IMMIGRATION AND AMERICANIZATION

References and Sources

Abbott, Grace, The Immigrant and the Community: Century, 1917.

Allen, Frances Newton Symmes, The Invaders: Houghton, 1913.

Anderson, J. T. M., The Education of the New-Canadian; a Treatise on Canada's Greatest Educational Problem: McBride, 1918.

Anthony, Joseph, Rekindled Fires: Henry Holt & Co.

Antin, Mary, They Who Knock at our Gates: Houghton, 1914.

Antin, Mary, Promised Land: Houghton, 1912.

Bacon, Robert, For Better Relations with our Latin-American Neighbors: Carnegie Endowment for Peace, 916.

Bailey, W. F., Slavs of the War Zone: Dutton, 1916.

Balch, E. G., Our Slavic Fellow-Citizens: Charities Pub. Co., 1910.

Bernheimer, C. S., Russian Jew in the United States: Winston, 1905.

Bridges, Horace J., On Becoming an American: Marshall Jones Co., 1919.

Bronsky, Amy, Illiteracy and Americanization: Wis. State Supt. Public Inst., 1917.

Bullard, Arthur, Comrade Yetta, by Albert Edwards (pseud.): Macmillan, 1913.

Burgess, Thomas, Greeks in America: Sherman French Co., 1913.

Cahan, Abraham, The Rise of David Levinsky: Harper Bros., 1917.

California Immigration and Housing Commission, Immigration Education Leaflets: Cal. State Printing Office, 1917.

Cather, Willa Sibert, My Antonia: Houghton, 1918.

Capek, Thomas, Slovaks in Hungary: Knickerbocker Press, 1916.

Chase, E. F., Bohemians: A Study of the "Land of the Cup and the Book,": Revell, 1914.

Clark, F. E., Old Homes of New Americans, Houghton, 1913.

Cohen, Rose, Out of the Shadow: Doran, 1918.

Commons, J. R., Races and Immigrants in America: Macmillan, 1882.

Coolidge, M. E. B. R. S., Chinese Immigration: Holt, 1909.

Dana, E. L., Makers of America: Im. Pub. Soc., 1915.

Dubnow, S. M., The History of the Jews in Russia and Poland; tr. from the Russian by I. Friedlander: The Jewish Pub. Soc. of America, 1918.

Fairchild, H. P., Greek Immigration to the United States: Yale Press, 1911.; Immigration: Macmillan, 1913.

Gabralian, M. C., Armenia, a Martyr Nation: Revell, 1918.

Goodman, F. T., City Government in the United States: Century, 1906.

Gordon, Charles William, The Foreigner, by Ralph Conner (pseud.), 1909.

Gordon, Winifred, Woman in the Balkans: Dodd, 1914.

Graham, Stephen, With Poor Immigrants to America, Macmillan, 1914.

Gulick, S. L., American Democracy and Asiatic Citizenship: Scribner, 1918; American-Japanese Problem: Scribner, 1914.

Hall, Prescott, Immigration and its Effect upon the United States: Holt, 1906.

Harley, J. H., Poland, Past and Present: Allen & Unwin, 1917.

Haskin, F. J., The Immigrant: Revell, 1913.

Hoben, Allan, The Church School of Citizenship: Univ. of Chicago Press, 1918.

Holt, Hamilton, Life Stories of Undistinguished Americans as told by Themselves: Pott, 1906.

Hourwich, I. A., Immigration and Labor: Putnam, 1912.

Hutton, Edward, Italy and the Italians: Dutton, 1903.

Jenks, J. W. & Lauck, W. J., Immigration Problem: Funk & Wagnalls, 1913.

Kellor, F. A., Straight America: Macmillan, 1916.

McClure, Archibald, Leadership of the New America: Doran & Co, 1916.

Miller, William, Balkans, Roumania, Bulgaria, Serbia and Montenegro: Putnam, 1908.
Nyburg, Sidney Lamar, The Chosen People: Lippincott, 1917. ,
Olmstead, Florence, Father Bernard's Parish: Scribner, 1916.
Ravage, M. E., An American in the Making: Harper, 1917.
Reade, Arthur, Finland and the Finns: Dodd, 1915.
Rihbany, Abraham Mitrie, A Far Journey; An Autobiography: Houghton, 1914.
Riis, Jacob, Making of an American: Macmillan, 1904.
Riis, Jacob, Neighbors; Life Stories of the Other Half: Macmillan, 1914.
Riis, Jacob, Children of the Poor: Scribner, 1892.
Riis, Jacob, Battle With the Slum: Macmillan, 1902.
Riis, Jacob, Children of the Tenements: Macmillan, 1903.
Riis, Jacob, How the Other Half Lives: Scribner, 1903.
Roberts, Peter, The New Immigration.
Ross, E. A., Changing America: Century, 1913.
Ross, E. A., The Old World in the New: Century, 1914.
Ross, E. A., Social Control: Macmillan, 1901.
Ross, E. A., Social Psychology: Macmillan, 1912.
Rudnicki, (Rudintsky), Stephan, Ukraine; the Land and its People: Rand, 1918.
Sartorio, Enrico C., Social and Religious Life of Italians in America: Boston, Christophar Pub. House, 1918.
Shriver, W. P., Immigration Forces: Missionary Education Movement of the United States and Canada, 1913.
Steiner, E. A., On the Trail of the Immigrant: Russell, 1906.
Steiner, E. A., Nationalizing America: Revell, 1916.
Steiner, E. A., Introducing the American Spirit: Revell, 1915.
Steiner, E. A., The Immigrant Tide: Revell, 1909.
Steiner, E. A., From Alien to Citizen: Revell, 1914.
Steiner, E. A., The Confession of a Hyphenated American: Revell, 1916.
Steiner, E. A., Against the Current: Revell, 1910.
Stern, E. G., My Mother and I: Macmillan, 1917.
Szlupas, John, Lithuania in Retrospect and Prospect: Lithuanian Press Assn. of America, 1915.
Talbot, Winthrop, Adult Illiteracy: Govt. Printing Office, 1916; Americanization: W. H. Wilson Co., 1917.
Taylor, A. H. E., The Future of the Southern Slavs: Dodd, 1917.
Tobenkin, Elias, The House of Conrad: Stokes & Co., 1918.
Towne, E. T., Social Problems; A Study of Present Day Social Conditions: Macmillan, 1916.
Tupper, E. W., Foreign-Born Neighbors: Tailor Press, 1914.
Villari, Luigi, Italian Life in Town and Country: Newnes, 1905.
Wald, Lillian, House on Henry Street: Holt, 1915.
Warne, F. J., Tide of Immigration: Appleton, 1906.
Warne, F. J., Immigrant Invasion: Dodd, 1913.
Warne, F. J., Slav Invasion and the Mine Workers: Lippincott, 1904.

Texts

Austin, Ruth, Lessons in English for Foreign Women: Amer. Book Co., 1913.
Beshgeturian, Azniv, Foreigners' Guide to English: World Book Co., 1914.
Chancellor, W. E., Standard Short Course for English Schools; Reading and Language Lessons for Evening Schools: Amer. Book Co., 1914.
Christoff, A. T., Practical Reader and Guide Book: Maunder-Dougherty Co., 1915.
Faustino, Madeline & Wagner, M. F., A New Reader for Evening Schools: Hinds, 1909.
Gield, W. S. & Coveney, M. E., English for New Americans: Silver, 1911.
Goldberger, H. H., English for Coming Citizens: Scribner, 1918.
Harrington, W. H. & Cunningham, C. J., A First Book for Non-English-Speaking People: Heath, 1904.
Harrington, W. H. & Cunningham, C. J., Language Lessons to Accompany the First Book for non-English-Speaking People: Heath, 1904.

Hill, M. H. & Davis, Philip, Civics for New Americans: Houghton, 1915.
Houghton, Frederick, First Lessons in English for Foreigners: Amer. Book Co., 1911.
Jimperieff, Mary, Progressive Lessons in English for Foreigners: Ginn, 1915.
Markowitz, A. J. & Starr, Samuel., Every Day Language Lessons: Amer. Book Co., 1914.
Mintz, F. S., The New American Citizen: Macmillan, 1909.
Mintz, F. S., A First Reader for New Americans: Macmillan, 1910.
O'Brien, S. R., English for Foreigners: Houghton, 1909.
Price, Isaac, Direct Method of Teaching English to Foreigners: Bealtys & Co., 1913.
Prior, Anna & Ryan, A. I., How To Learn English: Macmillan, 1911.
Richman, Julia & Wallach, I. R., Good Citizenship: Amer. Book Co., 1908
Turkington, G. A., My Country: Ginn, 1918
Wallach, Mrs. Isabel, A First Book in English for Foreigners: Silver, 1906.
Wallach, Mrs. Isabel, A Second Book in English for Foreigners: Silver, 1910.

Methods

Bagster-Collins, E. W., The Teaching of German in Secondary Schools: Macmillan, 1914
Berlitz, M. D., Methode Berlitz pour Conseignment des langues Moderns: M. D. Berlitz, 1918.
Brebner, Mary, Method of Teaching Modern Languages: Cambridge Univ. Press, 1909.
Breul, Karl, Teaching of Modern Languages and the Training of Teachers: Cambridge Univ. Press, 1909.
Goldberger, H. H., How to Teach English to Foreigners: A. G. Seiler, 1918.
Goldberger, Lesson Plan for Teachers. Pennsylvania Council of Defense; The Teaching of English to the Foreign Born: U. S. Bureau of Education.
Goldberger & Brown, Syllabus for Teaching English: Scribner's.
Gouin, Francis, The Art of Teaching and Studying languages: Longmans, 1892.
Handschin, C. H., Teaching of Modern Languages in the United States: Govt. Printing Office, 1913.
Jesperson, Otto, How to Teach a Foreign Language: Macmillan, 1914.
Mahoney, J. J. & Herlihy, C. M., First Steps in Americanization: Houghton, 1918.
Modern Language Association of America, Report of Committee of Twelve: Govt. Printing Office, 1899.
McDonald, R. A., Provisions for Modern English Speaking Immigrants: Columbia Univ., 1915

Pamphlets

Pamphlets and circulars may be obtained from the following departments and organizations:

Bureau of Education, Washington, D. C.
Bureau of Naturalization, Washington, D. C.
Council of Jewish Women, 146 Henry St., New York, N. Y.
Inter-Racial Council, 120 Broadway, New York, N. Y.
National Americanization Committee, 29 West 39th St., New York, N. Y.
National Catholic War Council, 930-932 14th St., Washington, D. C.
National Security League, 19 West 44th St., New York, N. Y.
North American Civic League, Boston, Mass.
Y. M. C. A.
Y. W. C. A.

BIBLIOGRAPHIES ON RACES IN AMERICA
Roumanians in America

Curtis, William Elroy, "Around the Black Sea": Doran, N. Y.
Kirke, Dorothea, Domestic Life in Roumania: John Lane, London.
Schierbrand, Wolf Von, Austria Hungary, the Polyglot Empire: Stokes, N. Y.
Seton-Watson, Robt. Wm. Racial Problems in Hungary: Constable, London.
Commons, John R. Races & Immigrants in America: Macmillan, N. Y.
Ravage, M. E., An American in the Making: Harper, N. Y.

The Slovaks in America

Balch, Emily Greene, Our Slavic Fellow-Citizens: Charities Pub. Committee, N. Y.
Capek, Thomas, The Slovaks of Hungary: Knickerbocker Press, N. Y.
Clark, Francis Edw., Old Homes of New Americans: Houghton, Boston.
Grose, Howard B., Aliens or Americans: Young People's Missionary Movement, N. Y.
Jenks, Jeremiah W. & W. Jett Lauck, The Immigration Problem: Funk & Wagnalls, N. Y.
McClure, Archibald, Leadership of the New America: Doran, N. Y.
Pergler, Chas., The Heart of Europe: Bohemian National Alliance, N. Y.
Seton, Watson, Robt. Wm., Political Persecutions in Hungary: Constable, London..
Seton, Watson, Robt. Wm., Racial Problems in Hungary: Constable, London.
Warne, Frank Julian, The Coal-mine Workers: Longman, Green Co., N. Y.
Warne, Frank Julian, Immigrant Invasion: Dodd, Mead Co.
Warne, Frank Julian, The Slav Invasion and the Mine Workers: Lippincott, Phila.

Bohemians (Czechs) in America

Capek, Thomas, Bohemia under Hapsburg Misrule: F. H. Revell, N. Y.
Balch, Emily Greene, Our Slavic Fellow-citizens: Charities Pub. Committee, N. Y.
Hodges, LeRoy, Slavs on Southern Farms: Wash. Government Printing Office, Wash., D.C.
McClure, Archibald, The Bohemians: Leadership of the New America.
Monroe, Will Seymour, Bohemia and the Czechs: L. C. Page & Co., Boston.
Riis, Jacob A., The Bohemian Tenement House Cigar Making; How the Other Half Lives, N. Y.
Stanton, Theodore, The Woman Question in Europe: Putnam's Sons.
Steiner, E. A., On the Trail of the Immigrant: F. H. Revell Co., N. Y.
Steiner, E. A., Among the Bohemians; From Alien to Citizen: N. Y.

Italians in America

Brandenburg, Broughton, Imported Americans: F. Stokes Co., N. Y.
Carr, John Foster, Immigrant & Library: Immigrant Publication Society, N. Y.
Garlanda, Frederick, The New Italy: G. P. Putnam's Sons, N. Y.
King, Bolton & Thos. O'KEY, Italy Today: J. Nisbet & Co., London.

Poles in America

Brandes, George, Poland: Heinemann, London.
Tucic, Sogjan Pl., The Slav Nations: Hodder & Stoughton.
Van Norman, Louis E., Poland, Revell, N. Y.
Winter, Nevin Otto, Poland of Today and Yesterday: L. C. Page, Boston.
Balch, Emily Greene, Our Slavic Fellow-Citizens: Charities Pub. Committee, N. Y.
Baskerville, Beatrice C., The Polish Jew: Macmillan, N. Y.
Clark, Francis Edw., Old Homes of New Americans: Houghton, Boston.
Hodges, LeRoy, Slavs on Southern Farms: Government Printing Office, Wash., D. C.
Jenks, Jere. Whipple & W. Jett Lauck, Immigration Problem: Funk & Wagnalls, N. Y.
Klenngott, George F., The Record of a City: Macmillan, N. Y.
McClure, Archibald, Leadership of the New America: Doran, N. Y.
Riis, Jacob August, How the Other Half Lives: Scribner, N Y.
Riis, Jacob August, Ten Years' War: Houghton, Boston.
Ross, Edw. Alsworth, The Old World in the New: Century, N. Y.
Shriner, Wm. P., Immigrant Forces: Missionary Movement of U. S. & Canada.
Stern, Eliz. Gertrude, My Mother and I: MacMillan, N. Y.
Thomas, Wm. Isaac and Florian Zraniecke, The Polish Peasant in Europe and America: University of Chicago Press.

Other Nationalities

Palmer, Francis H., Austro-Hungarian Life in Town and Country, Putnam, N. Y.
Harvey, Wm. J., Denmark and the Danes: J. Pott & Co.
Saivg, S., Observations on the Social & Political State of Denmark: Longmans, Green, London.
Daniels, H. K., Home Life in Noway: Methnen & Co., Ltd., London.

Heidenstam, Oscar, Swedish Life in Town and Country: Putnam's Sons, N. Y.
Ferriman, Z. Duckett, Home Life in Hellenes.
Monroe, Will Seymour, Bulgaria and Her People. L. C. Page & Co., Boston.
Rappoport, Angelo S., Home Life in Russia: Macmillan, N. Y.
Young, Ernest, Finland: Chapman & Hall, Ltd., London.
Garnett, Lucy M. J., Greece of The Hellenes: Sir. I. Pitman & Sons, London.
Miyatovitch, Chedomil, Servia of the Servians: C. Scribner's Sons, N. Y.
Palmer, Francis H., Russian Life in Town & Country: Putnam, N. Y.
Reade, Arthur, Finland and the Finns: Dodd, Mead & Co., N. Y.

BIBLIOGRAPHIES OF IMMIGRANT EXPERIENCES

Allen, Frances Newton Symes, The Invaders: Houghton.
Anthony, Joseph, Rekindled Fires: H. Holt & Co.
Antin, Mary, The Promised Land: Houghton, Mifflin Co.
Antin, Mary, They Who Knock at Our Gates: Houghton, Mifflin Co.
Berman, Henry, Worshippers: The Grafton Press.
Blaustein, David, Memoirs of David Blaustein: McBride, Nest & Co.
Bridges, Horace J., On Becoming an American: Marshall Jones Co.
Bullard, Arthur, Comrade Yetta by Albert Edwards: Macmillan.
Cohan, Abraham, The Imported Bridegroom and other Stories of the New York Ghetto: Houghton, Mifflin Co.
Cohan, Abraham, The Rise of David Levinsky: Harper & Bros.
Cohan, Abraham, Yekl; a Tale of the New York Ghetto: D. Appleton & Co.
Cather, Willa Sibert, My Antonia: Houghton, Mifflin Co.
Cather, Willa Sibert, O Pioneers!
Cather, Willa Sibert, Song of the Lark.
Cohen, Rose, Out of the Shadows: Doran.
Gordon, Chas. Wm., The Foreigner by R. Conner.
Hamsun, Knut, Shallow Soil: Scribner.
Hapgood, Hutchins, The Spirit of the Ghetto: Funk & Wagnalls.
Hasanovitz, Eliz., One of Them: Houghton, Mifflin Co.
Holt, Hamilton, ed., The Life Stories of Undistinguished Amercans: Pott.
Ireland, Alleyne, Joseph Pulitzer: Kennerly.
Irvine, Alex. Fitzgerald, From the Bottom Up: Doubleday.
McCall, Sidney, Sunshine Beggars: Little, Brown & Co.
Marcasscn, Isaac Fred, Autobiography of a Clown: Moffatt.
Miniter, Edith May Dow, Our Natupski Neighbors: Hoe.
Nyburg, Sidney Lauer, The Chosen People: Lippincott.
Olmstead, Florence, Father Bernard's Parish: Scribner.
Patri, Angelo, A Schoolmaster of the Great City: Macmillan.
Ravage, M E., An American in the Making: Harper & Bros.
Rihbany, Abraham Mitrie, A Far Journey, Houghton, Mifflin Co.
Steiner, E. A., Against the Current: F. H. Revell Co.
Steiner, E. A., The Confessions of a Hyphenated American.
Steiner, E. A., From Alien to Citizen.
Steiner, E. A., The Immigrant Tide.
Steiner, E A., Nationalizing America.
Stern, Eliz. Gertrude, My Mother and I: The Macmillan Co.
Tobenkin, Elias, The House of Conrad: Stokes & Co.
Tobenkin, Elias, Witte Arrives: Stokes & Co.

Printed in the United States
126123LV00004B/340/A

COLLIERVILLE BURCH LIBRARY   DUPL

3 8017 00062350 4